QUEEN MARGOT

Borgo Press Books by ALEXANDRE DUMAS

Anthony
The Barricade at Clichy; or, The Fall of Napoleon
Bathilda
Caligula
The Corsican Brothers (with Eugène Grangé & Xavier de Montépin)
The Count of Monte Cristo, Part One: The Betrayal of Edmond Dantès
The Count of Monte Cristo, Part Two: The Resurrection of Edmond Dantès
The Count of Monte Cristo, Part Three: The Rise of Monte Cristo
The Count of Monte Cristo, Part Four: The Revenge of Monte Cristo
A Fairy Tale (with Adolphe de Leuven and Léon Lhérie)
The Gold Thieves (with Countess Céleste de Chabrillan)
Kean
The Last of the Three Musketeers; or, The Prisoner of the Bastille
  (Musketeers #3)
Lorenzino
The Mohicans of Paris
Napoléon Bonaparte
Queen Margot
Richard Darlington (with Prosper Dinaux)
Sylvandire
The Three Musketeers (Musketeers #1)
The Three Musketeers—Twenty Years Later (Musketeers #2)
The Tower of Death (with Frédéric Gaillardet)
The Two Dianas (with Paul Meurice)
Urbain Grandier and the Devils of Loudon
The Venetian
The Whites and the Blues
The Widow's Husband; and, Porthos in Search of an Outfit
Young Louix XIV

RELATED DRAMAS:

The Queen's Necklace, by Pierre Decourcelle
The Seed of the Musketeers, by Paul de Kock & Guénée (Musketeers #5)
The San Felice, by Maurice Drack
The Son of Porthos the Musketeer, by Émile Blavet (Musketeers #4)
A Summer Night's Dream, Adolphe de Leuven & Joseph-Bernard Rosier
*The Widow's Husband; and, Porthos in Search of an Outfit: Two Dumasian
  Comedies*, edited by Frank J. Morlock

QUEEN MARGOT

A PLAY IN FIVE ACTS

ALEXANDRE DUMAS

Translated and Adapted by Frank J. Morlock

THE BORGO PRESS

MMXIII

QUEEN MARGOT

FIRST BORGO PRESS EDITION

Published by Wildside Press LLC

www.wildsidebooks.com

DEDICATION

To Conrad: yet another project that would never have seen the light of day without your support.

CONTENTS

CAST OF CHARACTERS

Henry of Navarre

Charles IX

La Môle

Coconnas

Duke d'Alençon

La Hurière

Caboche

De Mouy

René

Maureval

Friguet

Jailor

The Governor

A Huguenot

A Judge

Catherine de Medici

Marguerite

Madame de Nevers

Madame de Sauve

The Nurse

Jolyette

Gilonne

Mica

ACT I

SCENE 1

A square in Paris. To the right, the hostel of La Hurière with rooms opening on the street level, and on the first floor. To the left, the hotel of Admiral Coligny with a balcony. In the center, the dwelling of Moncey. On each side of this dwelling a street facing the audience and losing itself in the distance.

LA HURIÈRE

(at his door, seeing Maureval who enters from the left)

Ah! Come here, Lord Maureval, come here.

MAUREVAL

I am here!

LA HURIÈRE

Do you know who is there opposite us?

MAUREVAL

At the Admiral's home?

LA HURIÈRE

Yes, at the Admiral's—King Charles IX.

MAUREVAL

What of it?

LA HURIÈRE

What's he doing at the home of this anti-Christ?

MAUREVAL

By God! To give him the kiss of Judas. It is important that he suspect nothing. He is the God of those damned Huguenots and today he controls 10,000 swords, perhaps.

LA HURIÈRE

Then nothing is changed, despite this visit?

MAUREVAL

Nothing.

LA HURIÈRE

And is it still for tonight?

MAUREVAL

Without fail!

LA HURIÈRE

At what time?

MAUREVAL

No one knows yet; but a signal will be given us.

LA HURIÈRE

What will it be?

MAUREVAL

The tocsin will sound from Saint Germain.

LA HURIÈRE

The rallying sign?

MAUREVAL

The cross of Lorraine.

LA HURIÈRE

And the password?

MAUREVAL

Suise and Calais.

LA HURIÈRE

That's good; we'll prepare for the feast.

MAUREVAL

Quiet! Here's a tourist who's just come.

LA HURIÈRE

Pass this way.

MAUREVAL

Goodbye.

(La Hurière shows him through the house. Maureval can be seen leaving by a door which gives on another street. Coconnas enters on horseback, his eyes are fixed on a sign which represents a roast chicken and which bears the legend—To the Beautiful Tower.)

COCONNAS

By God! There's an inn which knows how to advertise itself, and the host must be, on my word, an ingenious chap. Besides, it's situated near the Louvre and that's where I'm going.

LA MÔLE

(arriving on horseback by another street)

On my soul, that's a pretty sign—then the hostel is near the Louvre; this will be my accommodation.

COCONNAS

(to La Môle)

By God! sir. I believe you and I both have the same feelings for

this inn—I congratulate myself for its flattering to my signory.
Are you decided?

LA MÔLE

As you see, sir—not yet, I am considering.

COCONNAS

Not yet? The house is still gratifying.

LA MÔLE

Yes, doubtless—this is a dainty painting, but that is exactly what
makes me doubt the reality. Paris is full of cheats, I am told, and
they can cheat with a sign just as well as with anything else.

COCONNAS

Oh! That doesn't worry me. I mock cheats. If our host furnishes
me with a bird less well roasted than that on his sign, I will
skewer him—and I won't stop until he's well done—that ought
to reassure you, sir.

(he dismounts)

Let's go in.

LA MÔLE

(dismounting in his turn)

You've finished by deciding me, sir. Sir—show the way, I beg
you.

COCONNAS

Ah! On my soul, I can't, for I am your humble servant, the Count Hannibal Coconnas.

LA MÔLE

And I, sir, am your devoted Count Joseph de Levac de La Môle—completely at your service.

COCONNAS

In that case, sir, let's lock arms and enter together. Say there, Mr. Host of the Beautiful Tower, Mr. Bumpkin, Mr. Clown.

LA HURIÈRE

Ah, excuse me, sir, I didn't see you.

COCONNAS

You must see us—it's your business.

LA HURIÈRE

Well, what do you want, gentlemen?

COCONNAS

(to La Môle)

He's better already, isn't he? Well, attracted here by your sign, we expected to find a supper and a bed in your hostel.

LA HURIÈRE

Gentlemen, I am in despair. There's only one free room in the hostel. And I fear you wouldn't like it.

LA MÔLE

Ah! My word, so much the better. We will go elsewhere.

COCONNAS

Not at all. Do as you please, Mr. La Môle, but I am staying. My horse is worn out—and I take the room—since you don't want it—besides, they positively told me about this hostel.

LA HURIÈRE

Ah! That's another matter. If you are alone—I cannot lodge you at all.

COCONNAS

By God, on my soul, a pleasant creature! Just now we were two too many. Now we are not enough for one. Look here, you don't want us to stay, comedian?

LA HURIÈRE

My word, since you take this tone, I will tell you frankly, I would much prefer not to experience the honor.

LA MÔLE

And why?

LA HURIÈRE

I have my reasons.

COCONNAS

Doesn't it seem to you we are going to massacre this character?

LA MÔLE

It's likely.

LA HURIÈRE

(sneering)

One can see these gentlemen have come from the provinces.

COCONNAS

And why's that?

LA HURIÈRE

Because in Paris, it's no longer in fashion to massacre innkeepers who refuse to rent their rooms. It's the great Lords who are massacred and not the bourgeois. Witness the Admiral, who yesterday received such a famous volley. And if you yell too loud, I am going to call the neighbors, and you will be beaten— treatment unworthy of two gentlemen.

COCONNAS

But this wise guy is mocking us, it seems to me.

LA HURIÈRE

Gregory—my arquebus.

COCONNAS

(drawing his sword)

Damn! Aren't you boiling, Mr. La Môle?

LA MÔLE

Not at all! For while we are boiling, our supper is freezing—

(to La Hurière)

My friend, for how much do you ordinarily rent your room?

LA HURIÈRE

A half crown a day.

LA MÔLE

Here are eight crowns for eight days. Have you anything else
to say?

LA HURIÈRE

My word, no—and with such manners. Come in, gentlemen,
come in.

(La Môle passes first, followed by Coconnas.)

COCONNAS

Even so! I have real trouble in putting my sword back in its scabbard before assuring myself that is has pricked the fat of this clown!

LA MÔLE

Patience, my dear companion! All the inns are full of gentlemen drawn to Paris by the marriage festivities and by the next war with Flanders. We probably couldn't find another room.

COCONNAS

By God! You've got cool blood, Mr. de La Môle. But let that rascal take care of himself! If his cuisine is bad—if his bed is hard—if his wine isn't three years old—if his valet is not supple like a reed—it will be my affair.

LA HURIÈRE

(putting away a large knife)

There, there, sir, you are in the land of Cocaine. Calm down.

(aside)

He's some Huguenot. These traitors are so insolent since the marriage of their Bearnaise with Princess Margot.

(smiling)

It would be funny if two Huguenots came to me today—St. Bartholomew's day—

COCONNAS

So, Count, tell me, while they are preparing our room for us, do you find Paris a gay city?

LA MÔLE

My word, no. It seems to me to have only frightening and surly faces—perhaps the Parisians are also afraid of the storm. See how black the heavens are—and how heavy the air.

COCONNAS

You will be going to the Louvre, right? After doing me the honor of conversing with me.

LA MÔLE

Yes.

COCONNAS

Well, if you like, while waiting for supper, we can find it together.

LA MÔLE

We could dine first?

COCONNAS

Not me! My orders are precise, to be in Paris on Sunday the 24th of August and go directly to the Louvre.

LA MÔLE

Let's go—so be it. It is well, says Plutarch, to accustom one's soul to sadness and one's stomach to hunger—

COCONNAS

You know Greek?

LA MÔLE

My word, yes. My preceptor taught me.

COCONNAS

By God, Count, your fortune is assured. You will compose verses with King Charles IX and you will speak Greek with Queen Marguerite.

LA MÔLE

Not to mention that I can still speak Gascon with the King of Navarre—are you coming?

COCONNAS

I'm with you.

(to La Hurière)

Finish up, here, master—what's your name?

LA HURIÈRE

La Hurière.

COCONNAS

Well, Master La Hurière, tell us the quickest way to get to the

Louvre.

LA HURIÈRE

Oh! My God—it's very easy—you follow the street to the church of Saint Germain—l'Axerrois—at the church you take a right and you are facing the Louvre.

LA MÔLE

Thanks.

(Coconnas and La Môle exit.)

LA HURIÈRE

(alone)

Hum! Now there are two gentlemen who seem to me to have the air of frightful freethinkers, I will recommend them to M. de Maureval—or rather since they are here—I will do my business myself.

(The Admiral's door opens.)

DE NANCY

(calling)

The King's litter!

LA HURIÈRE

Ah—King Charles the IX. He's leaving the Admiral's. O Great King, go. May God give you the prudence of the Basilisk and the strength of a lion.

THE KING

(leaning on the Admiral's shoulder)

Be easy, father, what the devil, when I give my only sister, Margot, to my cousin, Henry, I give her to all the Huguenots in the Kingdom. The Huguenots are all my brother's now.

ADMIRAL

(his arm in a sling)

Ah, sire, I don't doubt your intentions, but Queen Catherine—

THE KING

Coligny, I don't say this to anyone but you, but I can tell you, my mother is a mischief maker. With her, no peace is possible. These Italian Catholics only know how to exterminate each other. As for me, on the contrary, not only do I wish for peace, but I even wish to give power to those of the religion. The others are very dissolute, father. In truth, they scandalize me with their loves and misbehavior. Come, do you want me to speak frankly? I scorn all those who surround me—except for you and my brother-in-law from Navarre, this good little Henry, your student. I don't say your son for I am your son and I don't want you to have any other son but me.

(Enter the litter in which Catherine is hidden.)

ADMIRAL

Yet, sir, you have around you some brave captains and prudent counselors.

THE KING

No, God pardon me, you see, there's only you, father, only you who are brave like Julius Caesar, and wise like Plato. So, at the moment having war in Flanders, I truly don't know what to do—to keep you here as a counselor—or to send you there as a general. So, advise me—and who shall command? If you command—who shall advise me?

ADMIRAL

Sire, you must conquer first. Advice will come after the victory.

THE KING

Is that your opinion, father? Well, it will be according to your opinion. Tomorrow, you will part for Flanders and I will part for Amboise.

ADMIRAL

Your Majesty is leaving Paris?

THE KING

Yes, I am fatigued by all this noise and all these feasts. I am not a man of action—I am a dreamer—I wasn't born to be King, I was born to be a poet. The title of poet is the only one for which I am ambitious. So, I have already written to Ronsard to come join me in Amboise—and there, the two of us—far from noise, far from the world, far from bad men, under our great trees beside the river, to the murmur of brooks, we will speak of things of God—the only compensation there is in this world, for the things of man.

ADMIRAL

Sire, I can only applaud such a resolution, but Your Majesty will permit me, before your departure, to solicit an act of justice which is at the same time politic?

THE KING

Speak father, speak.

ADMIRAL

An act which will give a new security to the reformed religion.

THE KING

Speak—or rather you wish my full powers to accomplish this act?

ADMIRAL

No, sire, the example will be greater coming from you.

THE KING

Then tell me what is to be done?

ADMIRAL

(making a sign to a young man who steps forward from the crowd)

Allow me, sire, to present to you Monsieur de Mouy de Saint Phale.

DE MOUY

(a knee on the ground)

Sire, justice.

THE KING

Ah—you are the son of Captain de Mouy?

DE MOUY

Yes, sire.

THE KING

Who was traitorously killed by François Louviers de Maureval?

DE MOUY

Yes, sire.

THE KING

Rise then, sir. Justice will be done.

(The King gives him his hand to kiss.)

DE MOUY

Oh, sire.

ASSISTANTS

Long live the King!

ADMIRAL

Hear them, Sire!

THE KING

Thanks, brave people, thanks. But don't cry 'Long live the King' rather shout, Long live the Admiral'.

SEVERAL VOICES

Long live the Admiral!

THE KING

Goodbye, father—parting as we do, we belong to each other—body and soul.

(he embraces him)

Goodbye!

ADMIRAL

(wishing to conduct the King to his litter)

Sire, allow me—

THE KING

Not at all.

ADMIRAL

Sire.

THE KING

I wish it.

(The King gets into his litter. As the litter turns toward the audience, Catherine can be seen within, watching, listening attentively.)

THE KING

(low to his mother)

Are you pleased with me, mother? Have I played my role well?

CATHERINE

Yes, my son!

(The pages, the guards and the people leave with great acclamations.)

(The litter goes out.)

ADMIRAL

(discharging his gentlemen)

Well, de Mouy—you are satisfied, I hope?

DE MOUY

Yes—he seems to me in good faith.

ADMIRAL

Oh, I will answer for him as for myself.

DE MOUY

In any case, father, now that we can live in Paris in peace, if he doesn't do justice on the assassin for me, I will do it myself. Now, a brief word on another subject which touches me very closely and for me is no less important.

ADMIRAL

Speak.

DE MOUY

You persist in sponsoring Henry to us as the King of Navarre.

ADMIRAL

The throne belongs to him by right.

DE MOUY

Doubtless. But is he worthy of it?

ADMIRAL

Henry is worthy of all thrones, de Mouy.

DE MOUY

I can still attach myself to him.

ADMIRAL

As the ivy to an oak.

DE MOUY

But, you know, my attachment means absolute devotion.

ADMIRAL

Devote yourself frankly and completely then, for by devoting yourself to Henry, you are devoting yourself not only to a man, but to a cause—and this cause is the cause of the Lord.

DE MOUY

Then, in your opinion, he's the leader who can make the Huguenots strong and free, and the reformed religion great and strong?

ADMIRAL

He's the King who can do it, in the realm he governs, the first realm in the world.

DE MOUY

Then it's agreed, father. From today, he will dispose of me, as you would dispose of yourself. Goodbye.

ADMIRAL

Good and excellent young man.

(He follows him with his eyes and then reenters his hotel.)

(La Hurière arrives from the street. Coconnas is behind him.)

LA HURIÈRE

How they conspire. These Huguenots, for I am positive they conspire. Happily they won't be allowed to get away with it, for they would go very far indeed, but it is time to stop them. You are right, Mr. de Maureval, it is time.

COCONNAS

(tapping him on the shoulder)

Well, friend—supper?

LA HURIÈRE

By God—I had forgotten you, sir!

COCONNAS

What, you had forgotten me? And you admit it, clown?

LA HURIÈRE

My word, when you know why—and for whom—

COCONNAS

Why and for whom?

LA HURIÈRE

It was for His Majesty, Charles the IX, who just left—

COCONNAS

The King? By God! I am annoyed not to have seen him. The

King went by—in the street?

LA HURIÈRE

Yes, coming from the Admiral's house.

COCONNAS

What! The King went to visit that pagan?

LA HURIÈRE

(low)

Good! He's one of ours.

(aloud)

Gregory—quickly serve this gentleman. Serve! Serve!

COCONNAS

Well, it appears that he's humanizing—What's all this?

LA HURIÈRE

An omelette with bacon, so you won't have to wait, Your Lordship.

COCONNAS

Bravo!

(He sits down to eat.)

LA MÔLE

(entering by the other door)

Count, not only does Plutarch say in an aside, that one must harden one's soul to the sorrows of the stomach, but he also says further in another place, that he who has, must share with he who has not. For the love of Plutarch, will you share your omelette with me?

COCONNAS

Didn't you get to dine with the King of Navarre as you expected?

(offering him a seat)

LA HURIÈRE

Ah! It appears this one is a Huguenot.

LA MÔLE

No—the King of Navarre was not at the Louvre. But in exchange—

COCONNAS

Well—in exchange?

LA MÔLE

Oh—count—the adorable vision I have seen.

COCONNAS

A vision?

LA MÔLE

Try to imagine that through the offices of a young captain of the Reformed Religion, I was ushered into a large gallery, where, to my profound astonishment, there was no one about. There, my companion left me alone to discover for himself what was going on when suddenly a door opened and I found myself face to face with a woman so noble, so gracious, so resplendent, that at first I thought she was the ghost of the beautiful Diane de Poitiers who returns, they say—to the Louvre.

COCONNAS

And she was—?

LA MÔLE

She was quite simply the living Madame Marguerite, Queen of Navarre.

COCONNAS

My word, you are not unlucky—I prefer the living to ghosts.

LA MÔLE

You are right.

COCONNAS

And what did you say to this beautiful Queen?

LA MÔLE

Not a word. I was in ecstasy. I drew forth the letter I was carrying and gave it to her—and with the prettiest hand in the world, with the most slender fingers I have ever seen, and she slid the letter, still hot from my breast—into her satin corset.

COCONNAS

Oh—Oh—my companion how vividly you describe things.

LA MÔLE

I speak as I feel—and you, did you achieve your ends?

COCONNAS

By God—not everyone is favored like you by Gods and Goddesses. I luckily met a German—very agreeable for a German—we had nothing to say! But recognizing in me a good Catholic, he escorted me to Mr. de Guise—with whom I have some business.

(to Hurière who is entranced)

Well, what are you up to there? Are you listening to us?

LA HURIÈRE

(hat in hand)

Yes, gentlemen, I am listening—but to serve you. What can I do for you, sirs?

COCONNAS

Ah! Ah! The name of Guise is magic—as it appears, for from being insolent, you have become servile—Do you think my hand is less heavy than Mr. Guise, which has the privilege of making you so polite?

LA HURIÈRE

No, Count, but it is less long—besides—you must be told that the Great Henry is our idol—of Parisians like me.

LA MÔLE

Which Henry, if you please?

LA HURIÈRE

I only know of one.

LA MÔLE

Ah—but I, I know several. And there is one I invite you to your particular attention, my friend—not to speak ill of.

LA HURIÈRE

Which one?

LA MÔLE

His Majesty, King Henry of Navarre.

LA HURIÈRE

I don't know him.

(He makes a sign to Coconnas.)

LA MÔLE

Clown!

(He rises.)

COCONNAS

Now—what are you doing?

LA MÔLE

I am leaving the table, no longer being hungry.

COCONNAS

I am truly annoyed by that. I counted on waiting in your honorable company until the moment for returning to the Louvre.

LA MÔLE

You are returning to the Louvre?

COCONNAS

Yes, sir.

LA MÔLE

And I, too.

COCONNAS

At what time?

LA MÔLE

I have a rendezvous just about now.

COCONNAS

I, too.

LA MÔLE

Is that so! But do you know there is a strange link between our destinies? Where you come, I come; where you go, I go.

COCONNAS

In that case, listen—one cannot eat when one is no longer hungry but one can still drink when you're no longer thirsty. Let's drink until the time! And we will go to the Louvre together.

LA MÔLE

I ask your pardon—in agreeing to your invitation, I fear I might bring to the Louvre ideas not as clear as those expected of me. But who is our host talking with?

(La Hurière is seen on the street, very hot to speak with Maureval.)

COCONNAS

He's talking—the devil take me—he's talking with the same individual—

LA MÔLE

Huh? The same individual.

COCONNAS

Yes—with the same person he was already talking with when

we arrived—the man in the German cloak. Oh, oh, what fire he puts into it. Hey, say, Master La Hurière are you playing politics by chance?

LA HURIÈRE

(with a terrible gesture)

Ah—rogue!

COCONNAS

(rising and going to him)

What's wrong with you, my friend? Are you possessed?

LA HURIÈRE

(seizing the hand of Coconnas)

Silence! Wretch! Silence on your life!

COCONNAS

Oh! Oh!

LA HURIÈRE

Get rid of your friend, without losing a minute; we have to speak to you, this gentleman and I.

MAUREVAL

It must be done, do you understand?

COCONNAS

By God! It seems this is serious.

MAUREVAL

It cannot be more serious.

LA MÔLE

(from the house)

Well—what are you deciding?

COCONNAS

I think you are right, and it would be better for each of us to guard his own head.

(he reenters)

So—a last cup of wine. To your fortune.

LA MÔLE

To yours, sir.

COCONNAS

Are you retiring?

LA MÔLE

Yes, I am fatigued. It is only eleven o'clock—I have a rendez-vous at the Louvre at midnight—and I wouldn't be sorry to throw myself on my bed for an hour. Master La Hurière.

LA HURIÈRE

Count?

LA MÔLE

Escort me to my room, I beg you. Awake me at midnight. I will be completely dressed and ready quickly.

COCONNAS

Fine! Same as me. I am going to make all my preparations. Master La Hurière, give me some blank paper and scissors so I can cut off my seal.

LA HURIÈRE

But, wretch, you have still sworn?

(aloud)

Gregory, this gentleman asks for some blank paper and some scissors to trim the envelope! Come, Mons. de La Môle, come.

(He goes up the staircase, lighting La Môle.)

COCONNAS

(aside)

Decidedly, something extraordinary is happening here.

LA MÔLE

(going up)

Good evening, Monsieur de Coconnas. And good luck at the Louvre!

(La Môle and La Hurière go out. Maureval is at the far door.)

COCONNAS

Ah,—what have I just done?

MAUREVAL

What have you done, sir? You almost revealed, just now, a secret on which depends the fate of the realm. That's what you've done. From good fortune, God has willed that your mouth be closed in time by our worthy host. A word more and you would be dead. Now—we are alone, hear me.

COCONNAS

Just a moment, sir. Who are you, if you please, to speak to me with such a tone of command?

MAUREVAL

By chance, have you heard the name of the Sire Louviers de Maureval?

COCONNAS

The murderer of Captain de Mouy? Yes, doubtless.

MAUREVAL

Well, I am he.

COCONNAS

Oh! Oh!

MAUREVAL

Hear me carefully.

COCONNAS

By god, I believe I do! I am listening attentively.

MAUREVAL

Hush! Wait!

(He indicates a noise above his head. At the same moment, the room on the first floor lights up. La Môle enters with La Hurière.)

COCONNAS

It's nothing; it's my companion who's setting in.

LA HURIÈRE

(above)

Here's your room.

LA MÔLE

(above)

Marvelous! Don't forget to waken me at midnight.

LA HURIÈRE

Be easy!

MAUREVAL

Listen, the hour is striking—listen.

(The clock strikes, they count.)

COCONNAS

Eleven o'clock.

MAUREVAL

Fine! La Hurière is shutting the door. He's coming down. Come, master, come!

LA HURIÈRE

(returning)

We are alone. Let's have a seat.

MAUREVAL

Everything is carefully shut up?

LA HURIÈRE

Yes—and Gregory is standing guard outside. Are you there, Gregory?

GREGORY

(in the street)

Yes, master.

LA HURIÈRE

(to Coconnas)

Sir, are you a good Catholic?

COCONNAS

By God, since the day of my baptism, I have boasted so.

MAUREVAL

Sir, are you devoted to the King?

COCONNAS

Body and soul.

MAUREVAL

Then you are going to follow us.

COCONNAS

So be it! But, I warn you that at midnight, I have business at the Louvre.

MAUREVAL

That's exactly where we are going.

COCONNAS

I have a meeting with the Duke de Guise.

MAUREVAL

We do, too.

COCONNAS

I have a password.

MAUREVAL

We do, too.

COCONNAS

A personal sign of recognition.

MAUREVAL

We do, too. And wait, this will spare you the trouble of making a cross on paper.

(He pulls from his pocket three white crosses, giving one to La Hurière, the other to Coconnas and keeping the third for himself.)

COCONNAS

Oh, oh—this rendezvous, this word of the day—this rallying sign—is it for everybody?

MAUREVAL

Yes, sir—that is to say—for all good Catholics.

COCONNAS

There's a feast at the Louvre then.

LA HURIÈRE

Yes, and that's why I polish my helmet, I sharpen my sword and my knives—Gregory—come help me.

COCONNAS

(eyes starting)

Wait a moment! This feast it—is—?

MAUREVAL

You've been quite a while to figure it out, sir, and it's to be seen that you are not as tired as we are of the insolence of these heretics.

COCONNAS

But doubtless you have large numbers and powerful allies?

MAUREVAL

(escorting him to the window)

Do you see that troop passing silently in the shadow?

COCONNAS

Yes.

MAUREVAL

Well, the men who form that troop have, you can see, like La Hurière, you and I, a cross on their hats.

COCONNAS

Well?

MAUREVAL

Well—those men are Swiss from the smaller countries—loyal friends of the King. You see that other troop.

COCONNAS

The horsemen?

MAUREVAL

Do you recognize their leader?

COCONNAS

How can you expect me to do that? I've only been in town since five o'clock this afternoon.

MAUREVAL

Well, he's the one you have a meeting with at midnight at the Louvre. See, he's going there to wait for you.

COCONNAS

Duke de Guise.

MAUREVAL

Himself.

COCONNAS

But what are those other men doing who are going silently from door to door?

MAUREVAL

They are placing a red cross on the homes of the Huguenots and a white cross on those of the Catholics. In other times, we leave it to God to recognize his own, today we are more farsighted and we will spare Him the trouble.

COCONNAS

But they are going to kill them all then?

MAUREVAL

All.

COCONNAS

By order of the King.

MAUREVAL

By order of the King and the Duke de Guise.

COCONNAS

When?

MAUREVAL

When you hear the first clock, striking from Saint Germain l'Auxerrois.

COCONNAS

(explosively)

Ah! That will be very funny.

MAUREVAL

Silence! Now, it is useless to tell you, if you have some particular enemy—if he's not already a convert to the Huguenots—he will pass in the number.

(La Hurière during this conversation has armed himself from head to foot.)

MAUREVAL

Let's get going now.

LA HURIÈRE

Wait! Before putting ourselves on campaign status, let's assure ourselves of our own lodgers—as they say in wartime. I don't want my wife and children strangled while I am out. There's a Huguenot here.

COCONNAS

De La Môle?

LA HURIÈRE

Yes, that's the freethinker. He's already in the wolf's mouth.

COCONNAS

What! You are going to attack your guest?

LA HURIÈRE

It was with him in mind that I sharpened my rapier.

COCONNAS

While he's sleeping?

LA HURIÈRE

All the more reason!

COCONNAS

Oh! Oh!

LA HURIÈRE

You are saying!

COCONNAS

I say it's hard. de La Môle supped with me, and I don't know if I ought.

MAUREVAL

Yes, but de La Môle is a heretic, he is condemned, and if we don't kill him, others will kill him.

COCONNAS

That's true, but it doesn't seem to me to be a satisfactory reason.

MAUREVAL

Come, come, hurry up, gentleman, hurry up. A shot, a hammer blow, rapier thrust, a hit with a fire iron, however you wish—but let's finish it.

LA HURIÈRE

I'll go to his room and in a twinkle.

COCONNAS

Wait! I'll go with you.

LA HURIÈRE

What for?

COCONNAS

By God, I'm curious to see it done.

(He goes upstairs behind La Hurière.)

MAUREVAL

And I will wait for you. I also have something to do in the

meanwhile.

(he goes to the Admiral's door and marks it with a 2nd cross)

For this one here, better to put two crosses than one.

LA MÔLE

(rising)

What's that noise?

(He takes a pistol from the table.)

LA HURIÈRE

(listening at the door)

Eh! I think he woke up.

COCONNAS

It seems that way to me.

LA HURIÈRE

He's going to defend himself then.

COCONNAS

He's capable of it. Say, Master La Hurière, if he were to kill you—it would be funny.

LA HURIÈRE

Him! Him!

COCONNAS

I think you are drawing back.

LA HURIÈRE

Me? Get out! Drawing back? Never!

(He kicks on the door. He finds himself face to face with La Môle entrenched behind his bed with a pistol in each hand.)

COCONNAS

Now this is getting interesting.

LA MÔLE

Ah—he intends to murder me, so it appears! And is it you, wretch?

LA HURIÈRE

Monsieur de Coconnas you are witness that he has insulted me.

(La Hurière aims his arquebus and fires. The ball brushes by his head. La Môle aims.)

LA MÔLE

Help, Monsieur de Coconnas, help me!

COCONNAS

My word, de La Môle, the best I can do in this affair is not to put myself against you. Get out of it as best you can.

LA MÔLE

Ah—double traitors—since that's the way it is.

(He fires both pistols. Coconnas is struck in the left shoulder.)

COCONNAS

By God! I'm hit. Well then against us both since that's what you wish. Ah, I came with good intentions and you reward me with a ball in my shoulder—wait! Wait!

(drawing his sword)

LA MÔLE

(reaching an open window)

Murderer! Murderer!

(jumping out the window)

LA HURIÈRE

By God! He's getting away.

COCONNAS

Him! Wait.

LA MÔLE

(fleeing, pistol in hand)

Get the assassin!

COCONNAS

(pursuing him)

Get the Huguenot.

SEVERAL VOICES

Get the Huguenots! Kill! Kill!

(Several shots ring out.)

MAUREVAL

(to La Hurière)

Quickly—this will give the alarm to the Louvre—to the Louvre.

(Armed men run by. The tocsin sounds. Shots, shouting. Several wounded fall in the street.)

CURTAIN

ACT I

SCENE 2

Marguerite's room. Doors in the rear to the right and left. A window with shut curtains giving on a balcony—in the stage area a door to an office.

MARGUERITE

Well, who told you Madame de Nevers?

GILONNE

Doubtless, the Duchess didn't wish to confide her secrets to me for she sent this little note to Your Majesty.

MARGUERITE

Let me have it! .

(opening the letter and reading)

"My dear Queen, I had said, as you know, that this Kinglet of Navarre would be the happiest prince on Earth in becoming possessor of the most beautiful pearl in the crown of France. It appears I was wrong—Master Henry, as your brother King Charles calls him, has promised Madame de Sauve, that, if she would forgive his forced infidelity to sacrifice to her his first wedding night. Goodbye, dear Marguerite. Your mad but ever affectionate Henriette."—This is delightful.

(During the reading of the letter, the Duke d'Alençon has quietly come behind Marguerite. Gilonne wants to warn her mistress but the Prince forestalls her with a gesture and dismisses her.)

MARGUERITE

Impossible!

DUKE

And why's that? Henry's love for Madame de Sauve is not a secret, I think.

MARGUERITE

Ah, it is you, my brother?

DUKE

Yes.

MARGUERITE

You were eavesdropping on me?

DUKE

Yes.

MARGUERITE

(mysteriously)

On your own behalf or on that of our mother?

DUKE

On mine.

MARGUERITE

What did you want to know?

DUKE

If Henry was or was not my brother-in-law.

MARGUERITE

And where does that lead you?

DUKE

Who knows? Perhaps to learn if he will be King of Navarre—or not?

MARGUERITE

And what does it matter to you who are destined to become King of France?

DUKE

Yes, after the death of my brother, Charles. While waiting what do you expect? I am interested in the fate of this little Kingdom.

MARGUERITE

Well—are you satisfied? You see that the King won't come.

DUKE

I know it.

MARGUERITE

Then, since you've learned what you wanted to know—get out!

GILONNE

(reentering)

Madame—the King of Navarre is leaving his apartment and coming here.

MARGUERITE

The King of Navarre, you say?

DUKE

It appears we were mistaken.

MARGUERITE

Are you sure?

GILONNE

I saw him in the corridor preceded by two pages carrying torches.

DUKE

I congratulate you, sister.

(He goes toward the office door on the right.)

MARGUERITE

Now what are you up to?

DUKE

I am going to continue to inform myself.

MARGUERITE

You are going to listen to what will be said in this room?

DUKE

Yes.

MARGUERITE

Francois, I forbid you to do it.

DUKE

(threatening)

Take care, Marguerite! This time I am not just listening for myself.

MARGUERITE

And on whose behalf are you listening?

DUKE

On behalf of Queen Catherine.

MARGUERITE

(in consternation)

Ah.

DUKE

I knew quite well you were too submissive a daughter to oppose the will of our good mother.

(He goes into the office.)

MARGUERITE

(alone)

What is being plotted then, and what is going to happen? All day men with sinister faces have circulated in the Louvre. Could it be true, as rumor has said, there's to be a general proscription?

GILONNE

His Majesty, the King of Navarre.

(Henry enters with two pages carrying gold candelabra with red wax candles.)

HENRY

Well, Madame, my presence seems to surprise you. Weren't you expecting me?

MARGUERITE

Say rather, I no longer expected you!

HENRY

You were no longer expecting me?

MARGUERITE

Doubtless—didn't you yourself tell me that our union was a political pact, an alliance and not a marriage.

HENRY

All the more reason for me to come, if not to speak of love at least to speak of politics.

Gilonne, close the door and leave us.

MARGUERITE

Gilonne.

HENRY

You wish to keep Gilonne, Madame? So be it, and if she is not enough to reassure you, I can call your other women who are, without doubt behind that door.

(He takes a step toward the office.)

MARGUERITE

(hurrying forward)

No, it's not necessary and I am ready to listen to you, sir.

(low)

Gilonne leave us, but stay in the next room so I can call you if I need you.

HENRY

(aside, looking at the office)

There's someone there.

(aloud to Marguerite)

The door is indeed locked, right?

MARGUERITE

Yes, sir.

HENRY

We are quite alone?

MARGUERITE

Yes.

HENRY

Then let's have a talk.

(He points her to an armchair.)

MARGUERITE

As it pleases, Your Majesty.

HENRY

Madame, whatever people say of our marriage, I think it a good marriage. I am entirely yours and you belong to me.

MARGUERITE

I do not understand you, sir.

HENRY

Listen and you are going to understand me. Our marriage is a good marriage, we must consequently behave to each other as good allies, since we have sworn allegiance before God. Isn't that your opinion?

MARGUERITE

Doubtless, sir.

HENRY

I know, Madame, that you have great penetration. I know how the terrain of the court is strewn with abysses. But, I am young, and although I have never done harm to anyone, I have a good number of enemies. In what camp should I place the woman who bears my name and who has sworn affection to me at the altar?

MARGUERITE

Oh, sir, could you think—?

HENRY

I think nothing, Madame, I hope, and I wish to be sure my hope is well founded. It is certain, for you as for me, isn't it, that our marriage was only a pretext? Some are even more distant and they say that it was only a trick.

(Marguerite shivers)

Which of the two? The King hates me, the Duke of Alençon hates me, and Queen Catherine loathes my mother too much not to hate me a little.

MARGUERITE

Ah, sir, what are you saying?

HENRY

My most profound thoughts which I would hide if we were not alone. Didn't you tell me we were alone?

MARGUERITE

Yes, sir, I told you so.

HENRY

And that's exactly why I let down my guard, Madame, what makes me dare to tell you, I am not fooled—

(looking searchingly in her eyes)

Neither the caresses of King Charles, nor those of the queen mother, nor the Duke d'Alençon.

MARGUERITE

(excitedly)

Oh, sire!

HENRY

(aside)

It's the Duke d'Alençon. Very well.

MARGUERITE

Sir!

HENRY

Well? What's the matter?

MARGUERITE

It's that such talk is very dangerous.

HENRY

Not when a husband addresses his wife. Not when they are alone, and even if they were not alone, if he was speaking low enough so they could not be heard. I tell you indeed that I was threatened on all sides; threatened by the King, threatened by the Queen Mother, by the Duke d'Alençon, by the whole world. You know—one feels instinctively—danger shivers in the air, grazing you as it passes, and makes you shudder. It's what is called a presentiment. Well, against all the threats which may become outright attacks, I can defend myself with your help— for you are beloved precisely by all those persons who detest me.

MARGUERITE

Sir.

HENRY

Well, what's surprising about everybody loving you? Those I've just mentioned are your brothers and relatives. To love ones relatives and brothers is acting in accordance with God's heart.

MARGUERITE

But, still, what are you getting at? I am listening.

HENRY

At what I just told you. That if you are not my lover but my ally, I can brave everything, However, on the contrary if you are my enemy, Madame, then I admit to you in all humility, I am lost.

MARGUERITE

Me, your enemy? Never sir!

HENRY

But not my friend either, right?

MARGUERITE

Perhaps.

HENRY

And my ally?

MARGUERITE

Ah—your ally? Certainly!

HENRY

Your hand!

MARGUERITE

Here it is—and with an open heart.

HENRY

(kissing it and holding it in his)

Well, I believe you, Madame, and accept you as an ally. Then—let's understand each other fully—we were married without knowing each other—without loving each other—they married us without consulting us—we must become like husband and wife—you see, Madame, that I am going beyond your vows. But if, after this forced alliance we were to go freely, without anyone constraining us, if we were to go like two loyal hearts who owe each other confidence and mutual protection—do you see it this way, Madame?

MARGUERITE

Yes, sir.

HENRY

And it's a free alliance you promise me.

MARGUERITE

Yes, I swear to you!

HENRY

(casting a glance at the office)

Well, as the first proof of a loyal alliance and an absolute confidence—I am going to tell you the plan I have formed to combat, first off, the enmity of the Queen Mother, then that of King Charles, then that of the Duke d'Alençon.

MARGUERITE

Sir, I conjure you.

HENRY

What's wrong with you?

MARGUERITE

Nothing.

HENRY

I am going then—

MARGUERITE

Sir, let me breathe. It's so hot this evening—and this window—which is shut.

HENRY

Oh—you only meant that, Madame?

(aside)

I made no mistake. It's the Duke.

(going to the windows and opening it)

MARGUERITE

(following him)

Silence, sire—for pity on yourself.

HENRY

Didn't you assure me we were alone?

MARGUERITE

Eh, sir, who can answer for that when there are two doors to an apartment—or even when there's only one.

HENRY

Fine, Madame—you don't love me, it's true, but you keep your word.

MARGUERITE

What did you mean, sir?

HENRY

(low)

I mean if you were capable of betraying me, you would have let me continue since I was betraying myself alone.

(aloud)

Well, Madame, are you breathing more easily now?

MARGUERITE

Oh, yes, sire, much better.

HENRY

In that case, I won't bother you any longer. I owe you my respects, and some advances of good friendship. Please accept them as I offer them—with all my heart, go to sleep then—and good night.

MARGUERITE

So, it's agreed?

HENRY

(in the doorway)

Yes—a political alliance—frank and loyal.

MARGUERITE

Frank and loyal.

HENRY

(going, escorting Marguerite back)

Thanks, Marguerite, thanks—you are a true daughter of France. I part at ease, in place of your love, your friendship remains to me—I am counting on you as on your side, you may count on me—goodbye, Madame.

(Henry exits. As Marguerite returns, the Duke leaves the office.)

DUKE

Marguerite is neutral today. In eight hours, Marguerite will be hostile.

MARGUERITE

Did you understand?

DUKE

Me? Absolutely nothing. But who told you I needed to understand?

MARGUERITE

Brother, put off for a minute, I beg you, this cold and somber mask, which prevents looks from penetrating your thoughts, and tell me, tell me what's going on tonight?

DUKE

Tonight? Ask that of René?

MARGUERITE

What do you mean of René?

DUKE

Doubtless. He's a sorcerer, he will tell you. Good night,
Marguerite.

(He heads toward the door.)

MARGUERITE

Good night.

DUKE

(returning)

Ah—a bit of advice.

MARGUERITE

What?

DUKE

Before you go to bed, bolt each of your doors, and if you hear
some noise—put two bolts on.

(He leaves by the secret corridor.)

MARGUERITE

(alone)

What a wedding night!

MARGUERITE

Did Henry speak truly and our marriage is only a trick? If I hear some noise, as Duke d'Alençon's somber face said, put in a second bolt—I hear no noise. All is tranquil—no light on the horizon. The step of some late scholar—that's all.

THE VOICE OF A STUDENT

(singing in the street)

Why—
When I want to rustle your pretty hair
Or kiss your lovely mouth
Or touch your beautiful breast—
Do you hide away as if you were shut in a nunnery?
Why do you hide your eyes—
Your beautiful breast
Your face, your lips?
Do you want to save them for Pluto
Down in Hell, after Charon
Has taken his fare.

(The voice fades out.)

MARGUERITE

Everyone loves someone or something. I'm the only one who loves no one, and am loved by no one. He is right that I am queen.

(shutting the window)

Come Gilonne and get me ready to go to bed.

GILONNE

Madame.

MARGUERITE

What?

GILONNE

I can hear steps in the secret passage.

MARGUERITE

These steps cannot be those of my brother, Charles, or of the Duke d'Alençon or of my mother, Madame Catherine or of one of her women. Open and see.

GILONNE

Madame de Sauve!

MARGUERITE

Madame de Sauve.

MADAME DE SAUVE

Alas, yes, myself.

MARGUERITE

Have you come to find your lover even here, Madame? You know very well he's no longer here.

MADAME DE SAUVE

(on her knees)

Forgive me, Madame—oh, my God, I know to what degree I am guilty towards you—but injurious necessity—fear, terror, made me profit by this passage which was open to me as a lady of honor to the Queen Mother.

MARGUERITE

Get up, Madame, and as I don't think you came in the hope of justifying yourself to me, tell me why you have come.

MADAME DE SAUVE

Madame, hear me, in the name of heaven—and you may forgive me or scorn me later. Madame it's a question of life and death.

MARGUERITE

Of life and death?

MADAME DE SAUVE

Eh! Look at me, if it was a question of ordinary danger would I be so pale, so trembling, so lost? Would I even come to you?

MARGUERITE

What's going on then?

MADAME DE SAUVE

They are slaughtering the Huguenots—and the King of Navarre is the leader of the Huguenots.

MARGUERITE

Oh, my God. So that's the explanation of all these vague warnings—the realization of all these somber presentiments—but he—he is a king.

MADAME DE SAUVE

He runs more dangers than the others, Madame, for Queen Catherine has sworn his death.

MARGUERITE

His death? Why?

MADAME DE SAUVE

The predictions, they say, assure him the French Throne.

MARGUERITE

Oh—

MADAME DE SAUVE

All this has been done against the King of Navarre, everything was done to bring him to Paris—your marriage was only a snare.

MARGUERITE

And your love?

MADAME DE SAUVE

In a way. My love was ordered by the Queen Mother. Alas, she hoped that her orders were in agreement with my heart.

MARGUERITE

But to what end did she order you to love him?

MADAME DE SAUVE

So that he won't be your spouse, so that he will remain stranger to the King, and that the King, not having to struggle with your tears, can kill him. And that—on the night of your wedding he'd not be in your apartment for, in your arms, before your eyes, they wouldn't dare.

MARGUERITE

Ah, I understand, I understand what d'Alençon wanted to know. Where is he—where is he? The King of Navarre.

MADAME DE SAUVE

I don't know. I came to ask you. Where is he?

MARGUERITE

He left here just now. Oh, if I had known.

MADAME DE SAUVE

My God, what are we going to do? Pardon me, Madame. What are you going to do?

MARGUERITE

I am going to find Queen Catherine. The King of Navarre is under my protection. I promised him an alliance. I will be faithful to my promise.

MADAME DE SAUVE

But if you cannot reach the Queen Mother?

MARGUERITE

I will turn to my brother, Charles.

MADAME DE SAUVE

Go, Madame, go.

MARGUERITE

I am going.

MADAME DE SAUVE

Wait.

MARGUERITE

What?

MADAME DE SAUVE

The tocsin—the tocsin.

MARGUERITE

What does it mean?

MADAME DE SAUVE

It's the signal. Shouting.

MARGUERITE

Will they cut throats in the Louvre?

MADAME DE SAUVE

Eh! My God, yes.

VOICE OF LA MÔLE

(in the corridor)

Navarre! Navarre! Help!

MARGUERITE

Open, open, Gilonne!

MADAME DE SAUVE

It's not his voice.

(She leaves. La Môle enters without his cloak or hat; his doublet is torn.)

LA MÔLE

Madame—they are killing—they are butchering my brothers - they want to cut my throat, too. You are the Queen—save me!

(Falling on his knees before the Queen.)

MARGUERITE

My God! Who are you? What are you asking? Help? Help?

LA MÔLE

Madame, don't call. If they hear you, I am lost. The assassins are climbing the stairs behind me. I hear them—they are here!

(Coconnas, La Hurière, and a group of armed men.)

COCONNAS

Ah, by God—we have got him now.

LA MÔLE

(rising)

A weapon, a sword—a dagger let me defend myself.

COCONNAS

Here!

(He stitches him another blow.)

LA MÔLE

(pulling away)

Ah!

MARGUERITE

Wretches! Are you also going to murder a daughter of France.

LA HURIÈRE

Madame Marguerite!

COCONNAS

The Queen of Navarre! Madame, excuse us, but we are involved in the pursuit of a heretic.

MARGUERITE

Churches and royal castles are places of asylum. The Louvre is a royal palace. I order you to leave.

LA HURIÈRE

(to Coconnas)

Come! Come! We won't lack a good supply of others.

COCONNAS

Madame, it is the woman not the queen that I obey. Ah, cursed Provincial—if I ever get you again.

(He backs out slowly—still threatening.)

MARGUERITE

(after having heard the noise of steps going off)

They are gone! Where is this unfortunate?

GILONNE

Here.

MARGUERITE

Dead.

GILONNE

No—only fainted.

MARGUERITE

My God.

MARGUERITE

This is the young man who came to me earlier with a letter for the King. It's Mr. de La Môle.

LA MÔLE

(opening his eyes)

And you, you are the Queen. Ah, how beautiful you are, Madame!

MARGUERITE

Where to put him? In your room—Gilonne, in your room.

GILONNE

Wherever you wish, Madame.

MARGUERITE

Wait—someone's calling—

MADAME DE NEVERS

(outside)

Your Majesty, Madame Marguerite!

MARGUERITE

It's Madame de Nevers—it's Henriette. a last effort, sir—go in this office.

(running to the door)

This way, this way Henriette.

(turning)

Is he there? Yes—good.

(Gilonne leads La Môle into the office. Madame de Nevers enters followed by Halabardiers.)

MARGUERITE

Ah! You are not alone.

MADAME DE NEVERS

No—my brother-in-law the Duke de Guise has given me a dozen guards to escort me back to my hotel. I am leaving you six. For tonight, you may have need of guards from the Duke of Guise—

(to guards)

Install yourselves in this antechamber and obey Madame

Marguerite as you would me.

MARGUERITE

Oh! What a terrible night.

MADAME DE NEVERS

I don't find it so. I am a good Catholic.

MARGUERITE

Ah—if you knew, if you knew.

MADAME DE NEVERS

(reaching the other door)

Oh well—you can tell me all about it later.

(to her six guards)

Come.

(to Marguerite)

Goodbye.

(She leaves.)

MARGUERITE

How is he?

GILONNE

A little better.

MADAME DE NEVERS

(once again opening the door)

Madame.

MARGUERITE

What is it now?

MADAME DE SAUVE

They've just arrested him. They are taking him to the King.

MARGUERITE

I'm on my way.

MADAME DE SAUVE

Ah! You will never get to him. The orders are given.

MARGUERITE

Rest easy. I will find some way. Gilonne, I recommend this unfortunate to you—come, Madame, come.

MADAME DE SAUVE

Ah! May God protect Your Majesty.

CURTAIN

ACT I

SCENE 3

The arms room of the King. To the left, a large window with a balcony which can be used; from this window one can see the other bank of the Seine, the Tower de Nesle. Two doors to the right and left.

THE KING

(entering)

Where is Henry?

NURSE

(coming from her room)

Charles, my Charles, is it true what they say?

THE KING

And what do they say, nurse?

NURSE

They say they are massacring the Huguenots.

THE KING

Well—what difference does it make to you?

NURSE

But I am of the religion—

THE KING

Then hide yourself in some corner and pray to the God of the Huguenots that my mother doesn't find you.

NURSE

Charles!

THE KING

Enough. Call Mr. de Nancy.

(calling his dog)

Acteon! Come Acteon.

NURSE

Oh! My God! My God!

THE KING

Well—what did I say?

NURSE

(obeying)

Come, de Nancy, the King wishes to speak to you.

THE KING

Where is Henry?

DE NANCY

Arrested, sire, according to Your Majesty's orders.

THE KING

Where has he been taken?

DE NANCY

In the next room.

THE KING

Bring him in. Ah—now the hour has come—God will tell me one day if it has struck for my damnation or my salvation.

(Henry is brought in by de Nancy)

DE NANCY

Come in, My Lord.

(He brings Henry in and then retires.)

HENRY

(looking around him)

He is alone!

THE KING

Ah, it's you?

HENRY

Yes, Sire.

THE KING

(drying his face)

By God—you are pleased to find yourself near me, aren't you, Little Henry?

HENRY

Doubtless, sire, for I always am pleased to find myself near Your Majesty.

THE KING

More pleased than to be down there, huh?

HENRY

Where's that, sire?

THE KING

On the street.

HENRY

Sire, I don't understand.

THE KING

Look and you will understand.

(He opens the window and shows him the quays lit by torches and gunfire.)

HENRY

But, in the name of heaven, what's going on tonight?

THE KING

Tonight, sir, they are relieving me of all the Huguenots. You see that smoke and flame down there, above the Hotel de Bourbon? That's the smoke and flame of the Admiral's house—which is on fire. Do you see the body that good Catholics are dragging on a torn mattress? It's the body of the Admiral's son-in-law—of your friend, Teligny.

HENRY

(seeking his sword)

And disarmed! Disarmed!

THE KING

Looking for your sword? And what would you do with your sword?

HENRY

I don't know, sire, but I'd like to have it.

THE KING

Senseless! Haven't you understood what I said?

HENRY

No.

THE KING

I said I no longer wish Huguenots around me. Do you understand, Henry? I said—I no longer want them. Am I the King? Am I the master?

HENRY

But Your Majesty.

THE KING

My Majesty kills and massacres at this moment all who are not Catholic. It's my pleasure. Are you Catholic or Huguenot?

HENRY

Sire, recall your own words, "What does it matter the religion of those who serve me well?"

THE KING

Ah! Ah! Ah! Let me recall my words! Verba volent, as my sister Margot says. Yes, yes, they serve me well, the Huguenots, very well even. They slip and slide everywhere in all ranks, in all employments in finances, in shipping—in war—just as one, more bold than the others slides into my throne. But tomorrow, there won't be any more Huguenots. You hear, Henry? Tomorrow there won't be a single one left.

HENRY

Yes, sire, I hear.

THE KING

But do you understand?

HENRY

Marvelously.

THE KING

And you don't respond.

HENRY

In fact, Sire, I am responding.

THE KING

Well, and what do you respond?

HENRY

In that case, I don't see why the King of Navarre would do what those unlucky gentlemen who, to remain free of perjury, did not do—for they are unlucky—having to die because, having had proposed to them what is being proposed to me, they refused as I refuse.

THE KING

(grasping his arm)

Ah—yes, indeed, you think I have taken the trouble to offer the Mass to those whose throats are being cut down there?

HENRY

Sire, won't you die in the religion of your fathers?

THE KING

Yes, by God! And you?

HENRY

(tranquilly)

And I too, sire.

THE KING

Ah! So it's like that?

(grabbing his arquebus)

Do you want the Mass, Little Henry?

(Henry keeps silent.)

THE KING

Death, Mass or Bastille. Choose! Death—Mass or Bastille. Are you Catholic or Huguenot?

HENRY

I am your brother, sire!

THE KING

Damnation. This cannot pass—I have to kill someone.

(He runs to the window, aims at a man fleeing on the quay and fires. The man falls.)

HENRY

Oh—my God! My God.

CATHERINE

(raising the tapestry)

Well, is it accomplished?

THE KING

No—a thousand devils—no! The blockhead refuses.

(Catherine, looking around her, sees Henry leaning against the tapestry.)

CATHERINE

Then—why is he alive?

THE KING

He's alive—he's alive—because he is my brother.

HENRY

Madame—all this proceeds from you and not from King Charles. I see that now. It's you who determined this fatal union! It's you who had the idea of bringing me into a trap—me and my companions! It's you who conceived of making your daughter the bait in the trap to destroy us all. It's you who just now, separated me from my wife so that she wouldn't have the burden of seeing me perish before her eyes.

(Marguerite enters through the nurse's door.)

MARGUERITE

Yes—but it won't happen. They won't kill the husband before his wife's eyes, I hope.

HENRY

Marguerite.

THE KING

Margot.

CATHERINE

My daughter.

MARGUERITE

Sir, your last words accuse me and you are at once both right and wrong. Right, for I am, in effect, the instrument which has served to destroy you all—wrong, for I was unaware that you marched to your perdition. But, since I have learned of your danger, I remember my duty and I hurried here and thanks to the good nurse of my brother, I got in—so here I am—and the duty of a wife is to partake in the fortune of her husband—if you are exiled, sir, I follow you in exile—if you are imprisoned, I am a captive, if you are killed—I die.

THE KING

Ah—my poor Margot, you would do better to tell him to become a Catholic.

MARGUERITE

Sire, believe me, for your own sake—don't ask such a cowardly thing from a prince of your house. Think of it—you have made him my spouse.

THE KING

In fact, Madame, Margot's right and Little Henry is my brother-in-law.

MARGUERITE

Yes, brother-in-law! Yes. You spoke rightly. Charles. Give the husband to the wife. You won't make me a widow on the day of my marriage? Give me his life! I demand the life of Henry—on my knees.

THE KING

Well—take him away.

MARGUERITE

Thanks, brother. Thanks.

(to Henry)

Come quickly, come.

HENRY

But I, too, must thank.

THE KING

(low)

You can thank me later. Go! Don't you feel the boards trembling under your feet? Go!

(Shouts can be heard and fleeing Protestants can be seen. The King closes the window and falls into a chair. Henry and Margot leave.)

THE KING

Mother—there's a lot of blood being shed. Do you think God will forgive me?

CATHERINE

No—for this blood will have been shed uselessly if Henry keeps the blood he has in his veins.

THE KING

So—it was really against him alone that all this butchery was directed?

CATHERINE

Sire, you think yourself a great politician and you are only a child.

(She leaves.)

NURSE

Don't listen to her, Charles! You have done the right thing.

(She kneels on one side. The dog, Acteon, comes to lick his hand on the other.)

THE KING

These are perhaps the only two creatures on earth who won't curse me tomorrow.

CURTAIN

ACT II
SCENE 4

Henry's apartment, simply furnished, hangings in skins. Two doors in the rear.

HENRY

(alone)

Come on, come on, everything's calm. Three days have passed and I am still among the living. Again one must believe in miracles. It was indeed very lucky that they had the nice idea of killing me with iron or lead, instead of simply poisoning me—as they did my poor mother with perfumed gloves—and as they intended to do to de Condé with a sweetened apple. Decidedly, my brother, Charles, is not so bad a devil as Master René, and it's better to do business with the King of France then the Queen Mother's perfumer. It's also necessary to say that Marguerite has faithfully kept her word to me and she came in time.

Without her, I don't know how it would have ended. If indeed it is finished. I look at myself, I pinch myself. I feel a little more sure I am alive. But tomorrow—but tonight—in one hour, could I say as much? Now, who is this man disguised as a Swiss Guard—for he's not a soldier, who presented arms when I went by just now and said, "health to the King of Navarre." I turned. I didn't have time to see him—only I heard him. Ah! Ah! It seems someone is in the corridor. I hear footsteps; they are coming from this side—it's someone searching, hesitating—they're knocking—who is it?

A VOICE

(outside)

Milord it's a worker from the harness room who is bringing you the saddle you asked for.

HENRY

Me? I never asked for a saddle, my friend. You are mistaken.

VOICE

No, sire, I am not mistaken, I assure you.

HENRY

It seems to me I recognize that voice—let's open up.

(opening the door)

What do you want, and who are you?

DE MOUY

A friend, sire.

HENRY

A friend in this outfit?

DE MOUY

Otherwise, I would not have been able to get near Your Majesty.

HENRY

But still—

DE MOUY

Do you recognize me?

HENRY

De Mouy.

(nervously)

Do you absolutely wish to speak to me?

DE MOUY

I must, sire.

HENRY

Come in then.

(closing the door)

DE MOUY

Oh—fear nothing, sire, no one has recognized me and we are alone.

HENRY

No one has recognized you! Are you sure? We are alone! Can you answer for that?

DE MOUY

I answer for everything, sire.

HENRY

So you're still living, my poor friend.

DE MOUY

Yes, and it's not the fault of this infamous Maureval.

HENRY

My friend, don't speak ill of friends of the Queen Mother.

DE MOUY

You don't want me to curse my father's assassin?

HENRY

(low)

Do I curse René, the poisoner of my mother?

DE MOUY

Sire, you are King and doubtless God makes you stronger and wiser than other men. But, look, sire, let's be brief for the time is short and let's be frank because circumstances press us.

HENRY

Well, since you absolutely wish to, speak, my brave de Mouy.

DE MOUY

It is true that Your Majesty has abjured the Protestant Religion?

HENRY

It's true.

DE MOUY

With your lips or your heart?

HENRY

One is always thankful to God when he gives us life—and God has visibly spared me in a cruel danger.

DE MOUY

Sir, let's confess one thing.

HENRY

What?

DE MOUY

It's that your abjuration is an affair of calculation, not of conviction. You abjured so the King would let you live—and not just because God saved your life.

HENRY

Whatever may be the cause of my conversion, de Mouy, I am no less Catholic.

DE MOUY

Yes, but will you always remain so? At the first opportunity of regaining your liberty, won't your conscience return, too? Well, the occasion presents itself, La Rochelle is in revolt; La Roussillon and Bearn only wait a word to act, In Guyenne everyone is for war; Navarre awaits you. It's only a question of you getting to Navarre. Just tell me that your conversion was forced, sire, and I will answer for the future.

HENRY

No one can force a gentleman of my birth de Mouy—what I've done, I've done freely.

DE MOUY

But, Sire, think that in acting thus, you are abandoning us, betraying us.

(Henry remains impassive.)

DE MOUY

Yes, you betray us—for more than 500 Huguenots instead of fleeing have remained in Paris with the object of freeing you and providing you an escort until we reach some safe place belonging to our brothers, and everything is ready, understand clearly, Sire, to give you not only liberty, not only power, but a throne once more.

HENRY

(making an effort over himself)

De Mouy, I am safe, de Mouy, I am Catholic, de Mouy, I am the spouse of Marguerite, the brother of King Charles, the Duke of Anjou, and the Duke of d'Alençon—I am the son-in-law of my mother-in-law Catherine. De Mouy, in taking these diverse positions, I have calculated the chance and also the obligations.

DE MOUY

In whom can we believe then, sire? They told me your marriage with Madame Marguerite has not yet been consummated, they told me that you renounced through pressure, they told me the hate of Madame Catherine, already demonstrated against your mother, will never be satisfied until demonstrated on her son. They told me—

HENRY

Lies, lies, de Mouy! They have impudently deceived you. This dear Marguerite is indeed my wife, this Good Catherine is indeed my mother and my brother, King Charles, is indeed the master of my life and my heart.

DE MOUY

So this, Sire, is the response I shall take to my friends? I will tell them that while they repress us, King Henry holds the hand and gives his heart to those who butcher us! I will tell them that the King of Navarre has become the flatterer of the Queen Mother and the friend of Maureval and René. For the first time in my life, I fear, truly, of not being believed.

HENRY

(to Gilonne who enters)

Ah—Well, what's the matter, my good Gilonne?

GILONNE

A letter from Her Majesty, the Queen of Navarre.

HENRY

Oh, let me have it, let me have it, Gilonne. Thanks! Is there a reply?

GILONNE

I don't know.

HENRY

If there is a reply, I will bring it myself.

(Gilonne leaves.)

HENRY

You see de Mouy, on what terms we are with this dear Marguerite, when we cannot see each other, we write each other.

DE MOUY

Sire, at least make this sacrifice to your former popularity—of not risking any public act which will prove to our brothers that you have abjured. Sire, this ought to be easy for you.

HENRY

(reading)

"Don't fail to come on a pilgrimage to the pine tree. It must be done." You've come at the wrong time, my poor de Mouy.

DE MOUY

How's that?

HENRY

Yes, you came to ask me for a proof of skepticism, at the very moment when God has just manifested himself by a miracle.

DE MOUY

What?

HENRY

In truth, don't you know yet? A pine tree in the cemetery of the Innocents which was bare since spring time, has bloomed since Saint Bartholomew's day. Such a thing has not been seen in the memory of man, and it's proof, at least they say so at the Louvre, that the Lord viewed with pleasure what happened on that day. A pilgrimage is to be made to the place of the pine tree. My brother, Charles, has asked me if I would go—I haven't answered yet. You understand, I am too new a Catholic to fail in such an invitation. I recall just now that I did ask for this saddle from the harness shop. You were right to remove the emblem of the House of Bourbon, and to leave only the Fleur de Lys of France. When one is not King, when one does not especially wish to be, it's better not to wear royal arms!

Goodbye, De Mouy—you will tell this to the harness shop, right? As for me, I am going to Madame Marguerite—adieu.

(Henry leaves.)

DE MOUY

(alone)

(watching stupefied as Henry leaves, wrenching his hat in his hands, then throwing it at his feet)

Oh, by death, I didn't come here to listen to such words. This is the man that Coligny answered to me for as for himself whom I gave my life and my honor! By my word as a gentleman, it's a wretch of a prince; and I really want to kill myself here to besmirch him forever with my blood.

(Duke of d'Alençon enters from the door at the rear.)

DUKE

Hush—Mr. de Mouy; for someone besides myself might hear you.

DE MOUY

Monsieur d'Alençon! I am lost!

DUKE

On the contrary! Perhaps you've even found what you were looking for. Believe me, a blood as generous as yours can be better employed than reddening the sill of the King of Navarre.

DE MOUY

(astonished)

Milord, if I have understood correctly, Your Highness wishes to speak to me?

DUKE

Yes, de Mouy, but not in this room. They might hear us.

DE MOUY

Where do you want me to go, Milord?

DUKE

To my apartment. Leave by the other door and I will rejoin you in the corridor.

CURTAIN

ACT II

SCENE 5

The apartment of Madame de Nevers in the Hotel de Guise.
Rich hangings, doors to the left, right and rear.

MADAME DE NEVERS

Your Majesty can enter in complete safety, here we are free.

MARGUERITE

First of all, and above everything else, My Majesty begs you to
forget Her Majesty. You say then you are free, dear Henriette.

MADAME DE NEVERS

Oh! My God, yes: Neither brother-in-law nor husband, nobody!
Free like the air, like a bird, like a cloud. I go, I come, I command.
Ah! Poor Queen! You are not free—and you are sighing.

MARGUERITE

My dear friend, permit me to tell you, you are very gay for just
being free.

MADAME DE NEVERS

Your Majesty forgets that she has promised me to broach some confidences.

MARGUERITE

Again, My Majesty! We are annoyed, Henriette. Have you forgotten what's agreed between us?

MADAME DE NEVERS

No: Your respectful servant before the world, your mad confidante when we are alone; right, Madam? Right, Marguerite?

MARGUERITE

Yes, yes—that's more like it.

MADAME DE NEVERS

Neither our family rivalries nor perfidies of love—all open and frank, an alliance, offensive and defensive with the sole end of seizing in its flight, if we can catch it, this ephemeral thing called joy.

MARGUERITE

Right, my duchess, that's it.

MADAME DE NEVERS

Then what's new?

MARGUERITE

Isn't everything new for the last three days?

MADAME DE NEVERS

Oh, I am speaking of love, not politics. When we get to Lady Catherine, your mother's age—then we will play politics. But we are twenty, my beautiful Queen, let's talk of something else. Let's see, would you be married for all the world?

MARGUERITE

To whom?

MADAME DE NEVERS

Ah—truly you reassure me. It hasn't happened yet.

MARGUERITE

Entirely to the contrary, my poor Henriette, I am less married than ever.

MADAME DE NEVERS

My God! As one of my friends says, you are really happy.

MARGUERITE

You know someone who says 'My God'.

MADAME DE NEVERS

Yes.

MARGUERITE

And who is this person?

MADAME DE NEVERS

You always question me when you are the one who should speak—finish and I will begin.

MARGUERITE

Well—so be it, Henriette. I have a scruple.

MADAME DE NEVERS

A scruple about what?

MARGUERITE

Religious. Do you see a difference between the Huguenots and the Catholics.

MADAME DE NEVERS

In politics?

MARGUERITE

Yes.

MADAME DE NEVERS

Without a doubt.

MARGUERITE

But in love?

MADAME DE NEVERS

My dear friend, we women are such pagans that instead of joining sects, we admit all; instead of making gods—we thank several.

MARGUERITE

There's only one, right?

MADAME DE NEVERS

Yes—who has a quiver, a blindfold and wings. By God—long live devotion.

MARGUERITE

You push it a little further than that.

MADAME DE NEVERS

How's that?

MARGUERITE

You throw stones at the heads of Huguenots.

MADAME DE NEVERS

Let's do well and leave talking. Is that the end of your confidences, Madam?

MARGUERITE

One moment. It's that, if the stone my brother Charles spoke of was historical.

MADAME DE NEVERS

Well?

MARGUERITE

Well, I would abstain—

MADAME DE NEVERS

Good! Now I understand your scruple. He's a Huguenot?

MARGUERITE

Who?

MADAME DE NEVERS

Who? Our gentleman.

MARGUERITE

You've understood it's a question of a gentleman?

MADAME DE NEVERS

Truly, how difficult it is.

MARGUERITE

Henriette, be persuaded of one thing—it's that this gentleman is nothing to me and never will be anything.

MADAME DE NEVERS

No matter, he exists, right?

MARGUERITE

Yes, but he nearly failed to exist.

MADAME DE NEVERS

And how did you meet him?

MARGUERITE

In the midst of the massacre, having no other protector in Paris than the King of Navarre, he sought refuge in my apartment.

MADAME DE NEVERS

Where the King of Navarre didn't happen to be, of course.

MARGUERITE

You know it better than anyone.

MADAME DE NEVERS

And where he remains.

MARGUERITE

He was so grievously wounded, that I didn't dare to—

MADAME DE NEVERS

I understand that, but you know it's very worrisome, a wounded Huguenot in the times which we find ourselves? And what will you do with your wounded Huguenot, who is nothing to you and never will be anything?

MARGUERITE

I've made him a convalescent who lives in my office, and whom I intend to save, that's all.

MADAME DE NEVERS

He's handsome, he's young, he wounded, you are hiding him in your office, you wish to save him. This Huguenot would be a real ingrate if he's not very thankful to you.

MARGUERITE

He is already—and I'm afraid more than I wish.

MADAME DE NEVERS

And he interests you, this poor young man?

MARGUERITE

Oh—only for the sake of humanity.

MADAME DE NEVERS

Ah! Humanity, my poor Queen. It's always that virtue that destroys us women.

MARGUERITE

Yes, and you understand, as from one moment to the next, the King, d'Alençon, the Queen mother, my husband even, can come into my apartment.

MADAME DE NEVERS

You want to beg me to keep your little Huguenot so long as he's sick, on the condition that I return him when he gets better?

MARGUERITE

Comedian! No, I swear to that I am not preparing things so far in advance—only if you could find a way to hide this poor boy, if you could protect the life I saved him. I confess to you that I would be very thankful to you. You are free in the Hotel de Guise, you said yourself, you have neither brother nor husband, to constrain you and what's more, I remember well, behind this room, you possess a large office like mine. Will you lend this office to me until my Huguenot is cured?—which is an affair of five or six days at most. Then you will open the cage and the bird will fly off.

MADAME DE NEVERS

There's only one difficulty dear queen—it's that the cage is occupied.

MARGUERITE

What! You've saved someone too?

MADAME DE NEVERS

Exactly, and that's what I replied to your brother when I spoke so low that you couldn't hear.

MARGUERITE

Ah, yes, truly—

MADAME DE NEVERS

Listen, Marguerite, it's a wonderful story, no less beautiful, no less admirable than yours. After having left the Louvre, the evening of St. Bartholomew, I was returning to the Hotel de Guise, and I watched a house being burned and pillaged when suddenly, I heard women shouting and men swearing. I came out on the balcony and at first I saw a sword whose fire seemed to light the scene all by itself. I admired this furious blade. I love beautiful things, so naturally I looked for the arm that made it flash, then the body to which the arm was attached. Then in the midst of screams, in the midst of blows, I distinguished a man and I saw a hero, an Ajax! I became enthusiastic. I encouraged him by voice and gesture. I shook at every blow that threatened him. I breathed at each lunge that he made. It was, you see, my queen, the emotion of a quarter of an hour, that I'd never experienced, that I never believed to exist—so I was there, breathless, suspended, mute, when suddenly my hero disappeared.

MARGUERITE

How's that?

MADAME DE NEVERS

Under a stone that an old woman had thrown at him. Then, like the son of Croesus, I got back my voice, I shouted for help. My guards came, took him, carried him off and then carried him to the office you are asking for your protégé.

MARGUERITE

Alas, I understand the story so well, for it is almost mine.

MADAME DE NEVERS

With this difference, that serving my King and my religion I don't need to send away Mr. Hannibal Coconnas.

MARGUERITE

His name is Hannibal Coconnas.

MADAME DE NEVERS

Yes—it's a terrible name, isn't it? Well—he is worthy of his name.

MARGUERITE

Then my protégé is refused at the Hotel de Guise? I am annoyed because it's the last place where anyone would look for a Huguenot.

MADAME DE NEVERS

Not at all. Bring him here—he will sleep in this room. Each will have his own.

MARGUERITE

I confess to you, I had counted on you so much my dear Henriette, that I brought him in advance.

MADAME DE NEVERS

He's here?

MARGUERITE

Below, in my litter.

MADAME DE NEVERS

Let him come up! Let him come up. Master Ambrose Paré will treat them both at the same time.

MARGUERITE

Oh, no, not Master Ambrose Paré, my brother's surgeon! Are you thinking of such a thing? No, I found another doctor who has miraculously saved de Bussy from the last sword blow he received.

MADAME DE NEVERS

You have confidence in him?

MARGUERITE

A great deal; for I've observed him. In less than three days he's brought my poor injured person back from death to life.

MADAME DE NEVERS

What do you call him?

MARGUERITE

You don't need to know that, dear friend.

MADAME DE NEVERS

No matter! I may have need of him in my turn and not just for Mr. Hannibal Coconnas.

MARGUERITE

He's called Master Caboche, besides you can see him if you like, he knows his patient is being brought here. This evening he ought to come. See to it, I beg you that he's brought to La Môle.

MADAME DE NEVERS

Ah, our Huguenot is called La Môle?

MARGUERITE

Yes—Lerac de La Môle from a great family in Provence.

MADAME DE NEVERS

You will see that in looking carefully, we will find some place that his ancestors reigned—which will be a great joy.

MARGUERITE

Why's that?

MADAME DE NEVERS

So it won't be a misalliance.

MARGUERITE

Madwoman!

MADAME DE NEVERS

Then you accept, right?

MARGUERITE

Doubtless.

MADAME DE NEVERS

Well, bring the patient up.

MARGUERITE

Gilonne.

(Gilonne appears.)

MARGUERITE

My dear Gilonne, have La Môle step up.

MADAME DE NEVERS

Will you allow me to check on the health of my Catholic?

MARGUERITE

Of course, that's a good hostess.

MADAME DE NEVERS

Mica.

(Mica appears.)

MICA

Madame?

MADAME DE NEVERS

How is it with the Count?

MICA

Better and better, Madam.

MADAME DE NEVERS

What's he been doing in my absence?

MICA

He's been eating a wing of pheasant.

MARGUERITE

Ah, it appears his appetite is reviving—that's a good sign.

MADAME DE NEVERS

And then?

MICA

He stretched out on his cushions and I think he's sleeping.

MADAME DE NEVERS

Marvelous!

GILONNE

(opening the door)

Madame!

MARGUERITE

Ah, fine, let him come in.

MADAME DE NEVERS

Wait, I will retire.

MARGUERITE

Why's that?

MADAME DE NEVERS

Oh, my God, at the moment of leaving you this poor young man—perhaps he may have something to tell you—Mica, a young man is going to stay in this room, wounded like the Count de Coconnas! I want you to take the same care of him as you do of the Count. Your Majesty will find me in my room. Come, Mica.

(She goes out.)

MARGUERITE

Crazy Henriette! But how she reads into the depths of one's heart with her madness! Let's see—come in, sir!

LA MÔLE

(enters, very pale)

Here I am, Madame.

MARGUERITE

The trip didn't tire you too much?

LA MÔLE

No, Madame, and the good care you've taken of me has unfortunately born its fruit.

MARGUERITE

Unfortunately! Explain yourself, sir. I don't understand you.

LA MÔLE

Oh, without doubt, if I hadn't miraculously gotten back my strength, you would not have, in seeing me so near to death, had the courage to exile me from your apartment.

MARGUERITE

My apartment was not a safe enough place to keep you—

LA MÔLE

(ardently)

Oh—who told you Madame, that I wouldn't prefer to die there than live elsewhere?

MARGUERITE

Clearly you're not so nearly over your convalescence as you think since this delirium takes you.

LA MÔLE

You take me, you mean to say, Madame, for since I saw you at the Louvre, alas, I have had no other thought except to be received as one of your followers, able to see you always and to belong to you forever.

MARGUERITE

Sir, servants of your age are too dangerous, at least in the eyes of the world, for a Queen of my age. I will find some other position for you.

LA MÔLE

So, Madame, I can hope that I will see you again? I have no need to fear that in leaving you, I will never see you again?

MARGUERITE

Hope, Monsieur de La Môle, I will take care not to deprive a poor injured man of hope. Hope is the best medicine that I know.

(after a moment of silence)

By the way—you are at the home of my friend Mme. de Nevers. In the next room there is a gentleman wounded during the night of St. Bartholomew. If, by chance, this poor man was of a different faith than yours—which is possible—for the entire time you live here, forget that you are a Huguenot.

LA MÔLE

Madame, I promise that the memory of all your bounties will efface every other memory.

MARGUERITE

Good, thanks! But it's getting late and I still have a few words to say to Henriette! Goodbye, La Môle.

LA MÔLE

Madame, Madame.

(falls to one knee)

Your hand.

MARGUERITE

There are two sorts of people one mustn't refuse anything—children and patients. Here, sir!

(She gives him her hand to kiss and leaves.)

(During the last scene and this monologue night comes on, little by little.)

LA MÔLE

(alone)

Oh, my beautiful queen! Ask for my blood, my life, my soul—ask anything of me, except not to love you anymore. For if you ask that, devoted as I am, I would rebel.

(putting his sword on an armchair and stretching out on the cushions)

But no, she's thought of everything. So, in advance, she was occupied with me—so while I did not dare to tell her that my life was attached to hers, she prepares for me this favor of seeing her always! Oh! Thanks, Madame, thanks! But I hear some noise, a door is opening—someone is coming.

COCONNAS

(leaning on his scabbard)

My word, I'm very pleased to have a neighbor. He can keep me company in my hours of solitude; Madame de Nevers says he's a charming boy. Ugh, ugh. I think my shoulder is hurting me more than my head, if it's not my chest, which is hurting me more than my shoulder.

LA MÔLE

This must be the gentleman the Queen spoke to me about.

COCONNAS

Sir.

LA MÔLE

He's probably talking to me.

COCONNAS

Sir, are you in this room, if you please?

LA MÔLE

Here I am!

COCONNAS

Ah! Ah! Did they warn you that you had me for a neighbor?

LA MÔLE

Sir, I know I have the honor.

COCONNAS

Ah! So much the better. Enchanted to meet you.

LA MÔLE

Sir, I am your servant.

COCONNAS

You are wounded, sir?

LA MÔLE

Very grievously, but they told me of an accident which befell you.

COCONNAS

Meaning I escaped being murdered.

(looking around him)

Where the devil will I find an armchair. The earth is shaking.

LA MÔLE

Sir, I am on an excellent cushion, if you care to share it with me.

COCONNAS

With the greatest of pleasure.

(sitting and throwing his sword behind the cushions)

There—fine! I am not yet very firm on my feet and when I stand up a long time, everything about me spins, it seems to me the earth is shaking. Cursed old woman! Do you understand it? She threw a twenty-pound pot of flowers on me from the third floor. Right on my head—fortunately, I've got a thick skull. I already had a scratch on my shoulder and a stab in the breast, but that was nothing in comparison. And you, sir, when were you wounded?

LA MÔLE

I, sir, I received a word cut in the breast and dagger's blow across my arm.

COCONNAS

And, being so badly accommodated you are already up. In truth, it as a miracle.

LA MÔLE

My word, yes, sir, and it's a homage to my doctor. I think I fell into Asclepias' bed, although the clown has more the bearing of a bohemian than a God. With several drops of a very agreeable tasting elixir, my word—with some massaging of my wounds—all is rather as you see, or rather as you don't see—but as you will see when someone brings us in a light.

COCONNAS

He's a clever rogue, your bohemian—or so it seems to me. And what's his name, if you please? It's good to know such a man in the times we live in.

LA MÔLE

He's called Master Caboche.

COCONNAS

And he lives—

LA MÔLE

Near the Innocents, I think. But he tells me that if I had need of him, he's very well known in Les Halls and I have only to pronounce his name and they will show me his dwelling.

COCONNAS

Master Caboche near the pillory—very fine. As for me, I have been treated by a stupid donkey.

LA MÔLE

What's his name?

COCONNAS

Master Ambrose Paré.

LA MÔLE

But he's the King's doctor.

COCONNAS

I pity the King—can you imagine as I told you just now, that I cannot get up because it always seems to me I am wearing this devilish pot of flowers on my head, so that at each instant I faint.

LA MÔLE

Well, sir, I, on the contrary am doing wonderfully, and I already feel strong enough to take on the fellow who assassinated me.

COCONNAS

And that would be just. Ah, sir, when you meet him, when you hold him under your hand disembowel him for me in the best fashion—you see I promised the fellow who injured me, I'd send him a little ball.

(touching his shoulder)

But how did this happen to you?

LA MÔLE

My word, sir, I had back luck. I was abominably betrayed by a man who, from his appearance, I judged to be a good companion.

COCONNAS

You see the rogue! Ah, you interest me, sir! For your story is like mine. And this traitor wounded you.

LA MÔLE

You will see. I arrived in Paris on St. Bartholomew's day.

COCONNAS

Right! Just like me.

LA MÔLE

I had, that evening, business at the Louvre.

COCONNAS

Again like me.

LA MÔLE

I tried to get lodgings nearby.

COCONNAS

Always like me—ah, sir, what sympathy!

LA MÔLE

I stopped in a nearby street before a sign of the most appetizing appearance, a sign as deceptive as the greeting of the host.

COCONNAS

I see this. He shunned you?

LA MÔLE

My word, little less. You will judge. At the same time another gentleman arrived.

COCONNAS

At the same time as you?

LA MÔLE

Yes.

COCONNAS

At this inn?

LA MÔLE

Yes—a big clown—striding figure, red hair, red mustaches who flashed agreeable white teeth, and with whom I supped because of his appearance.

COCONNAS

(recoiling)

Indeed!

LA MÔLE

Who, forcing friendship upon me, invited me to retire to my room. He had his plans, the wretch!

COCONNAS

You think so? And what were the wretch's plans?

LA MÔLE

By God—that's easy to figure out. He was the host's accomplice.

COCONNAS

What was your host's name?

LA MÔLE

His name is La Hurière. I will never forget his name, I promise you. This devil of a host shot at me, happily I had my pistols.

COCONNAS

Then, you fired on this devil of a host and instead of shooting him, like the clumsy fool you are, you shot his companion, right?

LA MÔLE

(rising)

Eh! Eh! What do you mean by this?

COCONNAS

It means, my dear little heretic, that you are the Count Lerac de La Môle, right?

LA MÔLE

And that you are the Count Hannibal de Coconnas, I believe.

COCONNAS

Who wanted to save your life and who you wanted to disembowel. Wait! Wait!

LA MÔLE

My sword—my sword! Ah, since I've met you once more.

(He runs to his sword.)

COCONNAS

Ah, since I've found you again.

(He runs for his.)

LA MÔLE

(his sword in his hand)

You haven't got your good Arquebus carrying La Hurière nor your dagger carrying Maureval.

COCONNAS

(his sword in his hand)

And you, we are going to see if you always have such fine legs as you had the other night, running to the Louvre. Where are you, if you please, Monsieur Comte de La Môle?

LA MÔLE

Over here, Monsieur Comte de Coconnas. Well, I am waiting for you.

COCONNAS

Ah! Ah!

(They fence.)

(Mica enters with Caboche, carrying a torch.)

MICA

This way, master, this way. Oh my God—Madame la Duchesse, Madame la Duchesse.

(She runs out calling.)

COCONNAS

Here, parry this.

LA MÔLE

This is for you, Monsieur le Comte.

CABOCHE

Good! It seems I arrived in time.

(Marguerite and Madame de Nevers run in.)

MARGUERITE

Gentlemen.

MADAME DE NEVERS

Gentlemen.

COCONNAS

Good—the Duchess.

(lowering his sword)

LA MÔLE

Madame Marguerite.

(lowering his sword)

COCONNAS

It's delightful—we will meet again.

MADAME DE NEVERS

(to Coconnas)

Not at all, if you please, Count.

MARGUERITE

(to La Môle)

De La Môle, what is this violence?

LA MÔLE

Don't you recognize him yet, Madame? It's the same one who at the head of a gang of assassins followed me right into the Louvre.

MARGUERITE

(to Coconnas)

Count, this is not the first time we have seen each other.

COCONNAS

It's true, Madame, I've had the honor.

MARGUERITE

Count, perhaps you owe me some apologies for the manner in which you presented yourself three days ago at the apartment of a queen.

COCONNAS

The fact is, Madame, if I had known I was entering your apartment—

MARGUERITE

Yes, you will have put your sword in its scabbard as La Môle has already done and as you are going to do.

COCONNAS

Madame.

MADAME DE NEVERS

Obey, Hannibal.

COCONNAS

I obey.

MARGUERITE

Now, sirs, listen carefully—you, Count Coconnas, you owe your life to Madame de Nevers.

COCONNAS

That's true.

MARGUERITE

You, La Môle.

LA MÔLE

Oh, without Your Majesty, I would be dead!

MARGUERITE

Then you have no right to refuse the first demand we make on you.

COCONNAS

Doubtless.

LA MÔLE

Oh, Madame, order! You know quite well I await your orders on my knees.

MARGUERITE

Your hand, Count Coconnas.

COCONNAS

Hum! Hum!

MARGUERITE

Your hand, Monsieur de La Môle.

LA MÔLE

(touching Marguerite's hand)

Oh with joy, Madame.

MARGUERITE

(to Coconnas)

Do you refuse me, Count?

COCONNAS

No, no—but—the flower pot—I, eh—by God I feel ill, that's all.

(bending and falling on his knees)

MADAME DE NEVERS

Yes, indeed. Help! Help! Weak as he still is, he's not able to stand up so long.

LA MÔLE

(excitedly)

Master Caboche, don't you still have that excellent elixir which you had me drink and which had such a good effect.

CABOCHE

I always have some on me.

LA MÔLE

Then let me have it.

CABOCHE

Here.

LA MÔLE

(to Mme. de Nevers)

Permit me, Madame—

(taking Coconnas in his arm he puts the flask to his mouth)

Count Coconnas—come to yourself.

COCONNAS

(sighing)

Ah.

MADAME DE NEVERS

He's reopening his eyes.

MARGUERITE

Good La Môle!

COCONNAS

What have you given me! It's as if someone made me drink life.

(recognizing La Môle)

And it's you who have done me this service. Again.

(he takes two or three drops)

By God! La Môle, if I get better, on my oath, you will be my friend.

LA MÔLE

With all my heart.

MARGUERITE

(breathing)

Ah!

MADAME DE NEVERS

Well, Master, what do you think of our two wounded?

CABOCHE

That in a week, they'll be better than they ever were.

MADAME DE NEVERS

You see then, dear Queen, everything's going to be fine!

CURTAIN

ACT II

SCENE 6

The Cemetery of the Innocents to the right, in the foreground, a large pine tree in flower. To the left, the door of a gothic edifice. Under the arch, several doors to dwellings.

La Hurière, Master Caboche, Friguet and a crowd shouting "Noel."

CABOCHE

(approaching and breaking a branch)

Yes, Master La Hurière, it's the truth of God—a pine in flower at the end of August—it's a miracle!

LA HURIÈRE

It was for this doubtless that this very morning King Charles and all the court came in procession to the Cemetery of the Innocents. Also, I left the Inn of the Beautiful Star to see once again this good King Charles who relieved us forever of the Huguenots.

CABOCHE

And you greatly aided in this rude work—Master La Hurière. I saw you, arms in hand.

LA HURIÈRE

Well, do you begrudge me that? I spared you the trouble, that's all.

FRIGUET

Tell us, Master Caboche, is it true what they say?

CABOCHE

What are they saying, my child?

FRIGUET

That you have ointments to cure all sorts of wounds, and that, for example, if you wanted to you could have reattached the head of Admiral Coligny, which he would bear like you and me, instead of being hung from the gibbet of Mont Faucon.

CABOCHE

Do you want to try it on yourself?

FRIGUET

Not at all, Master Caboche, not at all.

CABOCHE

(pulling his ear)

Not even the ear?

FRIGUET

No, no—I believe in confidence—let me go, Master Caboche, let me go.

(He goes toward the one rear followed by the group of the people. La Hurière laughs and applauds following them with his eyes.)

(Coconnas and La Môle enter from the rear.)

COCONNAS

The Quarter of the Halls—the Cemetery of the Innocents—this has the appearance of being what we see—it is every attractive.

LA MÔLE

My word—on my side, I think I see one that is not less extraordinary.

COCONNAS

Who?

LA MÔLE

(pointing to La Hurière)

See!

COCONNAS

First of all, it's not a thing—it's a man.

LA MÔLE

Yes, but what man?

COCONNAS

Master La Hurière.

(La Môle and Coconnas each place a hand on his shoulder)

Good day master!

LA HURIÈRE

(looking to the right)

Ah, Count Coconnas.

(looking to his left)

Ah, Count La Môle.

COCONNAS

You are not dead?

LA HURIÈRE

You are still alive?

COCONNAS

I saw you fall there, I heard the noise of the shot which smashed some bone of yours, I don't know what. I left you fallen in the river, bleeding from the nose and mouth.

LA HURIÈRE

All that is true, like the Evangelist, Monsieur de Coconnas but the noise you heard was that of the shot striking my helmet on which happily it flattened. But the blow was none the less violent.

(raising his hat)

Look! It took off all my hair.

COCONNAS

Ah—a fine head.

LA HURIÈRE

Ah! Ah! You are laughing. Then you don't have any bad designs on me?

LA MÔLE

No.

LA HURIÈRE

You pardon me?

COCONNAS

Yes—only we put one condition on this pardon.

LA HURIÈRE

Which is?

COCONNAS

Just that you direct us to the dwelling of a doctor called Master
Caboche who lives somewhere in this area.

LA HURIÈRE

This area? Indeed you could say on the spot.

COCONNAS

How's that?

LA HURIÈRE

Look—there he is in his doorway.

LA MÔLE

Indeed—it's him in person.

LA HURIÈRE

So then?

LA MÔLE

So then, as in leaving here we were, we are—planning a visit
to Master René, the Necromancer, and since your inn is on the
way—prepare your omelet.

COCONNAS

And don't spare the butter as you did the first time.

LA HURIÈRE

Rest assured, gentlemen, on my oath! I didn't expect to get off so cheaply.

(He escapes.)

COCONNAS

(coming forward)

Well, I'm damned.

LA MÔLE

Do you recognize him?

COCONNAS

Marvelously.

(going to Caboche)

My dear friend, permit me to tell you that you are the cleverest surgeon that I know.

(presenting his hand. Caboche draws back)

Well?

(Caboche greets him)

Take it!

CABOCHE

Thanks for the honor you wish to do me, sir, but it's probable that if you knew me, you wouldn't do it to me.

COCONNAS

My word, for my part, I declare that if you were the devil, I consider myself obliged to you for without you—at this hour—I would be dead.

CABOCHE

(lifting his hat)

I am not quite the devil, sir, but often people would prefer to meet the devil than to see me.

COCONNAS

Who are you then?

CABOCHE

Sir, I am Master Caboche executioner to the Provost of Paris.

COCONNAS

(withdrawing his hand)

Ah! Ah!

CABOCHE

You see!

COCONNAS

Not at all. I will take your hand or may the devil carry me off.

CABOCHE

Truly?

COCONNAS

Completely.

CABOCHE

There.

COCONNAS

More completely still.

(He gives him a hand full of gold.)

CABOCHE

(shaking his head)

I had much preferred your naked hand for I do not lack gold. But of hands which touch mine, quite the contrary. I put them very much out of work. Never mind. May God bless you gentlemen.

LA MÔLE

(approaching and giving him a purse)

Here, my friend.

CABOCHE

Thanks, sir.

COCONNAS

So, then, my friend, allow me to look at you.

CABOCHE

Oh—go ahead, sir.

COCONNAS

So, it's you who work the rack, the wheel and draw and quarter? Who break bones and chop heads? Ah! Ah! I am indeed easy to have made your acquaintance.

CABOCHE

Sir, what you say is not quite right for I don't do it all myself— just as you gentlemen have lackeys to do what you don't care to do, I have my assistants who do the dirty work and who dispatch the peasants. Only when, by chance, I have an affair with some gentlemen like you and your companion for example—well, then it's another matter, and I make it a point to attend to all the details myself—from first to last, so to speak, to put the matter delicately.

COCONNAS

(looking at his companion)

Eh! Eh! What do you say to that, La Môle?

(turning and laughing)

Well, Master, I will hold you to your promise and if my turn comes to mount the scaffold—only you shall touch me.

CABOCHE

I promise you that.

COCONNAS

And this time, this time, here's my hand in witness that I accept your promise.

CABOCHE

You hand without gold, your hand all alone.

COCONNAS

Yes, and I repeat, enchanted to have made you acquaintance.

(The Duke d'Alençon enters, wrapped in a cloak—follows Coconnas and La Môle with his eyes. A man accompanies him.)

JOYLETTE

(to Caboche)

They're asking for you inside, papa.

CABOCHE

I am coming.

COCONNAS

By God! What a beautiful child.

CABOCHE

She's my daughter.

COCONNAS

What do you call her, Caboche?

CABOCHE

Joylette.

COCONNAS

Will you let me give you a hug, my pretty child?

JOYLETTE

Ask my father, sir.

CABOCHE

Hug, sir, hug—perhaps it will bring her luck.

LA MÔLE

You are going to hug the daughter of an executioner?

COCONNAS

I would hug the devil's daughter, if she was pretty.

(embraces her)

After all, I shook hands with her father.

LA MÔLE

You've got more courage than I do.

COCONNAS

Thanks, my pretty child. Till we meet again, Master Caboche.

CABOCHE

Don't say "Till we meet again—say goodbye."

JOYLETTE

Who is this handsome lord, papa?

CABOCHE

A brave gentleman, my child, and one for whom you should pray.

(They go into the house.)

LA MÔLE

Well—there you are with a friend at the Paris marketplace.

COCONNAS

On my word, there's an old Piedmontese saying, "It's nice to have friends everywhere."

(They leave. The Duke d'Alençon points out La Môle to the man who accompanies him.)

DUKE

You see, cloak and cap, cherry colored—the doublet, black and gold. Cherry, white and gold trousers. Can one get an outfit like that for this evening?

MAN

Yes, sir.

DUKE

That's fine. At eight o'clock someone will be at your place and take it to de Mouy.

MAN

Should I accompany Milord to the Louvre?

DUKE

No—I have other orders to give you.

(They leave by different directions.)

(After a moment, the King, Queen Catherine, Marguerite, Madame de Sauve, Friguet and La Hurière enter with guards.)

FRIGUET

The King—the King!

LA HURIÈRE

Long live the King!

(to those who are around him)

Do you see—do you see the first one—the one who has a gold doublet braided in gold—it's King Charles, the King of the Catholics.

PEOPLE

Long live the King!

LA HURIÈRE

That one is Queen Catherine—she who did it—see de Maureval told me—he must know, the King's killer.

PEOPLE

Long live King Charles. Long live Queen Catherine. Long live the Mass.

LA HURIÈRE

Here's Queen Marguerite.

THE KING

Well—where is this flowering hawthorn which the people are taking so much about?

CATHERINE

There it is, my son, come to this side.

THE KING

Ah—yes indeed—

CATHERINE

Fall on your knees, my son, and even if you don't believe it's a miracle, look as if you do.

THE KING

I believe it, by God! And the proof is that I will erect on this very spot, a chapel to the St. Bartholomew that our predecessor Louis raised to the Innocents.

MADAME DE SAUVE

(to Marguerite)

Madame—hasn't he come yet?

MARGUERITE

I warned him—now, perhaps he has scorned my advice, you had better warn him yourself.

MADAME DE SAUVE

Oh—it's impossible. I am prevented his sight.

MARGUERITE

Then separate yourself from me.

MADAME DE SAUVE

Oh—yes—you are right, Madame—but you will excuse me— if new dangers—

MARGUERITE

You know that I am allied to the King of Navarre.

CATHERINE

(on her knees by the King)

My son, what did I tell you?

THE KING

You told me something, mama?

CATHERINE

I told you he wouldn't come.

THE KING

What's that?

CATHERINE

Henry.

THE KING

Ah, yes, it's true—where is Little Henry?

CATHERINE

At a sermon, doubtless.

THE KING

Margot!

MARGUERITE

My King calls me.

THE KING

Yes.

MARGUERITE

(aside, looking around her)

He isn't coming.

THE KING

Why isn't Little Henry here?

MARGUERITE

Sir, I left him ready to come. Something must have delayed him.

THE KING

He's wrong, he's wrong. The streets of Paris are not yet cold enough for a half a Catholic to venture alone—he had been in greater security in our company than where he doubtless finds himself at the moment.

MADAME DE SAUVE

(aside)

Oh, my God! My God!

CATHERINE

Well, my son, do you still say that Henry—?

MARGUERITE

Sire, listen, I seem to hear.

THE KING

What?

SEVERAL VOICES

To the Mass, Henry—to the Mass.

CATHERINE

There he is.

LA HURIÈRE

He came, the heretic.

THE SAME VOICES

To Mass—to Mass.

HENRY

(entering on horseback)

Gentlemen, I went yesterday—I am coming from one today—I will go again tomorrow. Damn, that seems quite enough.

THE KING

Where are you coming from, Henry? And why are you so late?

HENRY

Sire, you heard—from Mass. Passing before Saint Germain, I went in—I heard a very beautiful sermon. I expected to find Your Majesty.

THE KING

You will find, mother, that it's we who are at fault and that Little Henry is going to be a better Catholic than we are.

HENRY

Sire, that will not astonish me—for I've heard it said from the pulpit that the Lord prefers a sinner who repents to the wise man who never sins.

THE KING

And you repent?

HENRY

Sire, I am very certain that nothing is missing from my wardrobe but a rosary like to that which our good mother wears—so that all may see in me one of the most fervent Catholics in the realm.

THE KING

Mother, give your rosary to Little Henry—I would be very curious to see the King of the Huguenots say his rosary.

CATHERINE

Indeed, let's see if he will engage in dissimulation.

(looking for her absent rosary)

My son, I've lost it or someone stole it from me.

HENRY

Good thief!

(aloud)

Madame, I am content to recite my prayers alone as the Italians say—and as the Italians are the first among Catholics, God cannot fail to make me have taste seeing I am trying to resemble them.

PEOPLE

Long live the king—long live the Mass. Charity! Charity!

THE KING

Hear, good people, hear!

(he searches for his purse)

Ah, ah, mother—it appears my purse has gone to join your rosary. Damn, he's a bold fellow who steals the King's purse to see how good the King's police are.

HENRY

Sire, I would offer you mine—but some good Catholic thinking that new saints make the best miracles has appropriated it as a relic.

THE KING

(laughing)

Gascon.

HENRY

No, damn! It's that I have the honor to tell Your Majesty they took me for a true King and stole it!

PEOPLE

Long live the King! Noel! Noel!

(The procession marches off.)

CURTAIN

ACT III

SCENE 7

The apartment of the Queen of Navarre.

GILONNE

(looking to the depths of the corridor)

A cherry cloak, a white and gold doublet. A hat crowned by a white feather. On my oath, that's indeed him. This way—Monsieur de La Môle—over here!

DE MOUY

(a handkerchief on his face)

Over here, you say?

GILONNE

Yes, yes—you are expected.

DE MOUY

By whom?

GILONNE

Eh! You know very well—by a woman.

(The voice of Coconnas can be heard.)

VOICE

Eh! La Môle! La Môle! Where the devil are you then?

DE MOUY

(to Gilonne)

You see, I am pursued.

GILONNE

Come in, quickly then.

DE MOUY

Where?

GILONNE

In this office.

DE MOUY

My word! By the grace of God.

(goes in)

GILONNE

(shutting the door)

It was in time!

(Coconnas enters.)

COCONNAS

La Môle! By God—what's wrong with you. You ran as if all the devils in hell were at your heels.

GILONNE

Ah! It's you, Count Coconnas?

COCONNAS

My word, yes—and very out of breath! Have you seen La Môle?

GILONNE

(a finger to her mouth)

Hush!

COCONNAS

What?

GILONNE

He is there!

COCONNAS

We are then in the Queen of Navarre's apartment?

GILONNE

Yes.

COCONNAS

And I, who did not understand anything. It's fine—it's fine! Your very humble servant. I am going.

LA MÔLE

(at the door)

Coconnas.

COCONNAS

(stupefied)

La Môle! How did you get out?

LA MÔLE

How did I get out? What do you mean?

COCONNAS

I understand. There are two doors and you took a tour.

LA MÔLE

There are two doors—where?

COCONNAS

To this office?

LA MÔLE

What are you telling me?

COCONNAS

You don't, by chance, dare to try to convince me that you didn't go in here?

LA MÔLE

When?

COCONNAS

Five minutes ago.

LA MÔLE

You are mad.

COCONNAS

I am mad! Be our judge, Madame.

LA MÔLE

Speak!

COCONNAS

Didn't La Môle just now go in this office?

GILONNE

I thought so, at least.

COCONNAS

Damn! You told me so.

GILONNE

And I repeat it. For myself, I thought so. But perhaps I deceived myself, perhaps it was a gentleman dressed in the same way. I was ordered to admit a lord in a cherry cloak and a white doublet.

LA MÔLE

Well.

GILONNE

Do you know any one who has an interest to get in here in your clothes, Count La Môle?

LA MÔLE

No one—unless—Oh, my God!

COCONNAS

What?

LA MÔLE

Unless someone is taking my place. Would that be treason?

COCONNAS

Whatever you please, but I say I saw you enter here—or if it wasn't you, it was someone who bore a devilish resemblance to you.

LA MÔLE

On your honor, Coconnas?

COCONNAS

On my honor?

LA MÔLE

Then I am going to find out.

(He takes a step towards the door—Gilonne puts herself in front of him.)

GILONNE

Count de La Môle!

LA MÔLE

Let me pass, Madame, let me pass.

COCONNAS

Eh, by God! You are forgetting that you are in a Queen's apartment!

LA MÔLE

Oh! It little matters to me where I am! A man has taken my name—a man has taken my clothes. I must know who this man is!

MARGUERITE

(entering)

Ah, it's you, Monsieur de La Môle! But what's wrong with you and why are you so pale and shaking?

GILONNE

Madame, in spite of me, Count de La Môle was going to go in Your Majesty's apartment.

LA MÔLE

Madame, it's because I wish to warn Your Majesty that a stranger, an unknown, a thief perhaps—has introduced himself into your apartment with my cloak and hat.

MARGUERITE

You are mad, sir, for I see your cloak on your shoulders, and I believe, God pardon me! that I see your hat on your head.

LA MÔLE

(hat in hand)

Oh, pardon, Madame, pardon! It's not that, God is my witness, I lack respect.

MARGUERITE

No—it's faith.

LA MÔLE

What do you expect, where a man is in Your Majesty's apartment, when he introduced himself by taking my costume and
perhaps my name—

MARGUERITE

But this man is not here to speak to My Majesty.

LA MÔLE

And for who then has he come?

MARGUERITE

For the King of Navarre, my husband—I charge you de La Môle
to find him and bring him here—are you reassured?

LA MÔLE

Ah, Madame!

COCONNAS

(looking at them)

The devil take me if I would be content with such an explanation!

LA MÔLE

(to Coconnas)

Come, come! I am already enough at fault, Coconnas.

COCONNAS

(bowing)

Madame.

MARGUERITE

(stopping him)

When the King of Navarre is gone, come to me, La Môle—I have to speak to you.

LA MÔLE

Oh! I will return.

(The two gentlemen leave.)

MARGUERITE

(to Gilonne)

Now, let Mr. de Mouy enter.

GILONNE

Mr. de Mouy?

MARGUERITE

Yes—he is in my room. He's dressed as de La Môle.

GILONNE

De Mouy in Your Majesty's room.

(she opens and watches de Mouy enter)

In Mr. La Môle's costume. I don't understand a thing! Come in, sir.

MARGUERITE

Watch outside. Don't let anyone in except the King of Navarre.

(De Mouy enters. Gilonne goes out.)

MARGUERITE

So, Monsieur de Mouy, you refuse to acquaint me with your motive for visiting the Louvre this evening?

DE MOUY

Deign to excuse me, Madame, and do not insist on a response from me.

MARGUERITE

Listen, Monsieur de Mouy, I took you to be one of the strongest leaders of the Huguenot party—for one of the most faithful partisans of my husband, am I wrong?

DE MOUY

No, Madame, for up to a week ago, I was all you say.

MARGUERITE

And for what reason have you changed in a week?

DE MOUY

Madame, I must keep silent; and the duty I am under must be very real for me not to have already answered Your Majesty.

GILONNE

(rushing in)

His Majesty, the King of Navarre, Madame.

DE MOUY

Ah, the King of Navarre! Let me leave—

MARGUERITE

At this moment, it is impossible.

DE MOUY

Dare I observe to Your Majesty that if the King of Navarre sees me at this time, in this costume, in the Louvre, I am lost!

MARGUERITE

(showing him the curtain by the window)

Sir, behind this curtain, and you are well hidden there—better perhaps than in your house for you can be sure of my word.

(De Mouy hides.)

MARGUERITE

The King of Navarre is to renounce the throne! I had thought him more ambitious than that. Have I deceived myself? Let's see.

HENRY

Here I am, Madame, I rush at your call.

MARGUERITE

My calling you did not astonish you, sir?

HENRY

I admit that I did not expect so great a favor.

MARGUERITE

So great a favor? What's so surprising in a woman begging her husband to spend some time in her apartment?

HENRY

Between wife and husband, no—I find nothing surprising in that.

MARGUERITE

And between allies?

HENRY

It's true, between allies, that can also happen. You are right, Madame, and I, ingrate that I am, I am wrong to be surprised.

MARGUERITE

Fine, sire, and now that you're over this surprise let's sit down and talk.

HENRY

Let's talk—yes—but first—

(looking to the office)

Are we alone?

MARGUERITE

Absolutely alone.

HENRY

(aside)

Then there's someone hidden.

MARGUERITE

Sire, you recall the day of our marriage?

HENRY

(gallantly)

Do I recall it! Oh, surely, yes—the day I owed you my life—you see I would be very ungrateful if I didn't recall it.

MARGUERITE

There was nothing surprising about that, Sire—it was the result of a pact we made together. You haven't forgotten the pact?

HENRY

No, Madame.

MARGUERITE

Well, it's in the name of that pact, loyally entered into between two loyal hearts—that I want a frank and loyal reply to my question.

HENRY

I am very ready—ask—

(Marguerite casts a glance toward the window)

He's behind the curtain.

MARGUERITE

Is it true, sir, that Your Majesty consents to abjure—as is the public rumor today?

HENRY

What do you want, Madame! When one is twenty-five years old and so near King there are some things indeed worth a mass.

MARGUERITE

And life is one of the things, right?

HENRY

Eh! Eh! I don't say no.

MARGUERITE

And are you sure of achieving this end, sire—of saving your life?

HENRY

Almost, Madame. Although, you know, in this world no one can be sure of anything.

MARGUERITE

It's true that Your Majesty announces so much moderation, and professes such disinterest, that after having renounced his crown, and his religion, he'll probably renounce his alliance with a daughter of France.

HENRY

(after a moment of silence and quick glance at Marguerite)

Deign to remember, Madame, that at this moment I don't have complete free will. I will do as I am ordered by the King of France—as for me, if they consult me in this matter which goes no less to my wellbeing, my throne and my life—rather than depend for my future on these marriage rights—I would prefer to bury myself as a huntsman in some chateau or penitent in some cloister.

MARGUERITE

Your Majesty has no great confidence, it seems to me, in the star which shines on the face of Kings.

HENRY

It's that I've vainly sought mine, Madame, I cannot see it—hidden as it is by the storm which rages against me at this hour.

MARGUERITE

And if the breath of a woman could ward off this storm and make this star more bright?

HENRY

It's very difficult.

MARGUERITE

Do you deny the existence of this woman?

HENRY

No, I deny her power.

MARGUERITE

You mean to say her will?

HENRY

I said her power, and I repeat the word. A woman is not really powerful except when love and interest are united in her to an equal degree. If one of these emotions preoccupies her, then she is vulnerable. Yes, the woman who could ward off this storm knows that I cannot count on her love.

(Marguerite is quiet)

Listen. At the last stroke of the clock of St. Germain, you must have thought of regaining your liberty—as it was put in pawn—as it was put in pawn to destroy those of my party. I ought to have thought of it. It was most necessary. We are losing Navarre, I can see that clearly—but Navarre is a small thing in comparison to the life we keep.

MARGUERITE

Ah, it's too much!

HENRY

What is?

MARGUERITE

Ah, Sire, it's wrong what you are doing.

HENRY

What do you mean?

MARGUERITE

I mean that to reward my frankness with all these evasions is not keeping the word you gave me.

HENRY

Madame, I swear to you.

MARGUERITE

Don't swear—or, if you swear take an oath not to wear a mask
and that all you've just said is the truth and not a trick or a lie!

HENRY

(low to Marguerite)

Eh, by God! Madame—then swear to me no one is behind this
curtain.

MARGUERITE

(low)

Ah! Ah! Well played! Yes, sir, there is someone who is entirely
of my opinion and like me, I am sure, only waits for an opportunity to cast his life on your fortune.

HENRY

And I know this person?

MARGUERITE

Judge for yourself.

(She makes de Mouy come out.)

HENRY

De Mouy.

(low and excitedly)

Madame, do you think there's some way someone could hear us?

MARGUERITE

Sir, this room is cushioned and a double panel assures us of its deafness.

HENRY

I am in agreement with you. But, believe me, let's speak low. De Mouy, my brave de Mouy! Oh, how glad I am to see you!

DE MOUY

Sire, it's nothing you said in our last meeting—but my presence then, allow me to tell you, appeared less agreeable then than today.

HENRY

(shrugging his shoulders)

Child! You didn't understand—

DE MOUY

Sire, my wits are not very subtle and I humbly ask Your Majesty's pardon for it, but from what you told me, I only understand what you said and not what you wished to tell me.

HENRY

(to Marguerite)

Madame, who suggested that you bring me face to face with de

Mouy?

MARGUERITE

Sir, I guessed that you and Monsieur de Mouy should meet.

HENRY

Ah! You guessed that.

MARGUERITE

Yes.

HENRY

Do you understand, De Mouy? She guesses—

MARGUERITE

And now, when followed by this young man who took you for his friend, you entered this room, I hesitated—for a week ago, in the corridor of the Louvre in the very doorway of the King of Navarre—you gave your hand to Monsieur d'Alençon.

HENRY

You see indeed, de Mouy, she knows everything, Monsieur d'Alençon has gotten to you? Speak frankly, my friend.

DE MOUY

It's your fault, sire—why did you so obstinately refuse the throne of Navarre, which I came to offer you?

MARGUERITE

You refused the throne of Navarre? This refusal of which you just spoke to me has actually taken place?

HENRY

Oh, truly, Madame, and you my brave de Mouy, both of you make me laugh with your exclamations. What! A man named de Mouy, meaning a man that all the world is watching—this man enters my apartment, disguised as a worker in a harness shop—enters my room which is watched constantly, and shut up each night like a prison—he talks to me of reversals, of revolt, to me, Henry, a Prince by sufferance, provided that I bear a humble face, Huguenot-spared on the condition that I play Catholic—and he expects me to accept his proposals—made to me in a room I don't know, in a room not padded, in a room adjoining Monsieur d'Alençon! By God—you are children—or you are mad!

DE MOUY

But, sire, Your Majesty can't you give me some hope, if not by words, at least by a gesture, a sign.

HENRY

Wasn't the Duke d'Alençon waiting for you at my door?

DE MOUY

Yes, sire.

HENRY

What did I tell you?

DE MOUY

That, since you refused the realm of Navarre, he accepted it—

HENRY

Since he knew I refused it, he must have heard you offer it to me?

DE MOUY

Doubtless, he was listening.

HENRY

And he understood, you admit it yourself, poor conspirator that you are! If I had said a word, you would have been lost, for if I didn't know, I suspected at least that he was there and if not he, someone else, Charles, the Queen Mother. Oh, you don't know the walls of the Louvre, de Mouy, it's in their honor they coined the saying, "The walls have ears" and knowing these walls, should I have spoken? Come, come de Mouy, you do little honor to the good sense of the King of Navarre, and I am astonished that you didn't come to offer me a crown.

DE MOUY

But, I repeat, sire, can't you, while refusing this crown, give me a sign? I wouldn't feel so desperate—so lost.

HENRY

Eh! By God! If he heard, couldn't he also see? And isn't one lost by a sign as much as by a word?

(looking around him)

Look, de Mouy, at this time, between you and her, so close together as you are, and speaking so low that my words do not pass the circle of our three chairs, yet I still fear to be overheard when I say to you—de Mouy repeat to me this evening those propositions you made to me that morning.

DE MOUY

But, sire, now I am engaged to the Duke d'Alençon.

MARGUERITE

(striking her hands together)

Then it is too late.

HENRY

But, on the contrary, agree that it is exactly the protection of God is apparent. Remain engaged, de Mouy—for the Duke, France is our refuge. Do you think that the King of Navarre can guarantee our heads? You decree yourselves unfortunates. I will get you all killed. But a son of France, that's another matter. Ask, for proofs, De Mouy, ask for guarantees, but innocent, that you are, you have already engaged your heart and a word would have been enough for you; I see that indeed.

DE MOUY

Oh, Sire, it was the despair of your abandonment that threw me into the arms of the Duke. Also, it was the fear of being betrayed for he knows our secret.

HENRY

Fine! Hold his in your turn then, it depends on you. What does he want? To be King of Navarre? Promise him the crown. What does he intend? To leave the court? Furnish him the means to flee. Work for him, de Mouy, as if you were working for me. Direct the shield so it parries all blows that would fall on us. If he must flee, flee with him—if he must fight and reign, I will fight and reign alone.

MARGUERITE

Be careful of the Duke, Henry, he is a somber and penetrating spirit, without hate, without friendship—always ready to treat his friends as enemies, his enemies as his friends.

HENRY

And he's waiting for you this evening, you said, De Mouy?

DE MOUY

Well, sire, prepare to flee, prepare to fight, for the moment has come.

HENRY

How's that?

DE MOUY

That's exactly what I'm going to learn this evening from the Duke d'Alençon.

MARGUERITE

Speak, de Mouy, speak.

DE MOUY

You know that, tomorrow, he's hunting the length of the Seine, from Saint Germain just to Maisons—that is to say the entire length of the forest. It is from this circumstance that we have decided to profit, for it favors the flight if his Royal Highness.

HENRY

And His Royal Highness has decided to flee with you?

DE MOUY

Yes, for the principals of our religion who will be reunited tomorrow in the forest in the name of Monsieur d'Alençon, have warned me that they will no longer believe in anyone except in those who will come publicly to act and fight with them.

HENRY

Well, de Mouy, I will be there.

MARGUERITE

You, ah, then!

DE MOUY

Then, sire, be ready for tomorrow.

MARGUERITE

Am I not you ally, sire? Must I not share your good and your bad fortune?

DE MOUY

Then it's unnecessary for me to go to the Duke d'Alençon?

HENRY

Go there, on the contrary—de Mouy—it would awaken his suspicions if you were not to go. Let nothing change your plans until tomorrow. And until tomorrow let the name of the Duke d'Alençon alone be accredited among you as the future chief of your party.

(giving him his hand)

Thanks! You understand de Mouy: You have all night to make your preparations.

DE MOUY

Then, sire, you do not renounce the realm of Navarre?

HENRY

I renounce the realm—de Mouy, I reserve to choose the best.

DE MOUY

So be it, but listen, Sire—Monsieur d'Alençon, so that I can act without inconveniencing him, this evening sent me the costume of a gentleman named de La Môle, and it is this excess of precaution which, after having almost lost all, has saved us, for pursued by one of the friends of this gentleman who took me for him, I was obliged to take refuge in this apartment. Well— it's necessary that this young man who is moreover a Huguenot be one of us.

(At the name of La Môle, Marguerite leaves her seat, blushing and goes to sit a few paces away at her toilette.)

HENRY

Tell me, Madame, this La Môle, of whom de Mouy is speaking—isn't he the same one whose life you saved during the night of St. Bartholomew?

MARGUERITE

Yes, Sire.

HENRY

You heard what de Mouy said, Madame, we must have this young man.

MARGUERITE

Since such is your wish, sir, I will do my best to second it.

HENRY

Then hasten, de Mouy.

(de Mouy starts to leave)

Not that way. By this door. I will escort you—three raps on my door in passing will indicate nothing has changed, but in the name of heaven, don't try to see me.

(De Mouy exits.)

HENRY

As for you, Madame, I leave La Môle to you. Spare neither gold nor promises to seduce him. I put all my treasury at his disposition.

(Henry exits.)

MARGUERITE

(watching him aside)

Gold or promises! Poor La Môle. He will give me his life for less than that.

(calling)

Gilonne.

GILONNE

(appearing)

Madame?

MARGUERITE

Tell La Môle that he can enter.

(Gilonne goes out and returns with La Môle.)

MARGUERITE

Now that we are alone, let's have a serious discussion, my good friend.

LA MÔLE

Seriously, Madame?

MARGUERITE

Or intimately. Let's see, do you prefer that? There can be serious things in intimacy and especially the intimacy of a Queen.

LA MÔLE

Let's talk then—of serious things, but one the condition that Your Majesty, not be angry at the mad things I am going to say to her.

MARGUERITE

I desire, first of all, one of those mad things—and I am going to get there first. You are jealous of my handsome gentleman?

LA MÔLE

Oh—enough to lose my mind!

MARGUERITE

And jealous of whom? Let's see!

LA MÔLE

Of everybody! For, again, you are so beautiful that the whole world must love you.

MARGUERITE

And, in the first rank of those who love me, you place de Mouy.

LA MÔLE

Why else does he come here?

MARGUERITE

For Monsieur d'Alençon with whom he conspires.

LA MÔLE

But this white doublet—this cherry cloak—this so perfect disguise—that my best friend himself was deceived?

MARGUERITE

A ruse of my brother's, La Môle, so de Mouy can penetrate the Louvre without being recognized and consequently without compromising him—and me—I've known all this since—deceived like your friend I took him to be you at first. He has our secret, La Môle—he must be managed.

LA MÔLE

Oh—I prefer to kill him—that's the quickest and securest way.

MARGUERITE

And I, my brave gentleman, I much prefer that he live and that you know everything—for his life is not only useful to us, but necessary. Listen and carefully: weigh your words before answering me. Do you love me enough, La Môle, to rejoice if I become truly Queen—that is to say mistress of a true kingdom?

LA MÔLE

Alas, Madame, I love you enough to desire what you desire,

even if this wish ruined my entire life.

MARGUERITE

Noble heart! Yes, I accept your devotion and I know how to reward it.

(giving him her hands)

Well?

LA MÔLE

Oh—now Marguerite, I begin to understand. Yes, this real royalty of Navarre which must replace a fictitious royalty you lust after: King Henry pushes you that way—De Mouy conspires with you, isn't that right? But the Duke d'Alençon, what's his role in this affair?

MARGUERITE

The Duke, friend, conspires on his own account. Let's let him ruin himself, his life answers to ours. Well, La Môle, I await your response

LA MÔLE

Here it is, Madame, they pretend—and I have heard it said to the ends of France, where your name is so illustrious, your beauty so universally recognized and adored—came like a vague desire of unknown things to touch my heart—I have heard it said that you had loved—once—that you had loved often—and that your love always brought misfortune to the objects of your love—so much so that death, jealous, doubtless, had almost always taken your lovers from you. You sigh, my queen, your eyes are becoming veiled. So it's true. Well, let only one of your glances promise to make me happier and better loved then your favorites, and dispose of my life, my soul, my wellbeing. Only, you must swear to me that, if I die for you as a somber presentiment warns me—that if the executioner separates this head from the body you envelop in your arms, sweet necklace of love under which my entire body shivers. You swear to me right? That before it is thrown in a cold grave that before they entomb me in solitary tomb you will come—you, my Queen, to place a last kiss on my face, and bring to me, in this strange world what lives already in my soul—the price of my devotion, the reward of my martyrdom.

MARGUERITE

O Lugubrious madness—O fatal thought.

LA MÔLE

Swear.

MARGUERITE

Must I swear?

LA MÔLE

Yes.

MARGUERITE

Well, yes, if it please God that your somber presentiments are realized, my handsome gentleman, I swear it to you—dead, your memory will always be near me—as living your love had been—and if I cannot save you from peril—or you lose yourself for me alone, I will give at least to your poor soul the consolation that you ask, and that you will so well have deserved. La

Môle, by the living God, I swear it!

LA MÔLE

Well, madam, as I leave at this moment, you dispose not of your servant, nor your friend, but your slave. I am nothing more to myself—I am yours.

MARGUERITE

La Môle, I accept, and you will find in me a devotion like to the one you give me. La Môle, come before the hunt and you will learn what you must do. Goodbye, my handsome gentleman, goodbye.

LA MÔLE

Goodbye, Madame.

(Marguerite tenders her hand toward him. He raises it to kiss it, she leans towards his face and touches his lips with kisses, then she flees to her room.)

LA MÔLE

Marguerite!

(rising)

She loves me! Oh, thanks, Marguerite; for now I am no more a vulgar favorite, and I can carry this head high—for living or dead, it is reserved a sweet future.

(He leaves.)

CURTAIN

ACT III
SCENE 8

Catherine de Medici's apartment. In the rear, a chimney. Doors right and left. To the left a secret armoire and a window masked by tapestries.

CATHERINE

Six o'clock and René hasn't come!

(a knock at the rear)

Here he is.

(going to the door and opening it)

Why so late, René, who kept you?

RENÉ

Lovers, Madame, who were made happy by oath that they were loved in return.

CATHERINE

Master René, no secrets from me. It was my daughter, Marguerite, it was La Môle—what were they doing at your place?

RENÉ

You see this statuette, Madame.

(Pulling a wax doll from beneath his cloak.)

CATHERINE

Pressed to the heart, with a crown on its head—an 'M' on the shoulder belt, de La Môle is so amorous of the Queen of Navarre that he has to have recourse to magic.

RENÉ

Like a madman!

CATHERINE

Then this doll is worth keeping René.

(she puts it in the secret armoire)

We shall find it again the day we need it. Fine—have you completed the experiments I indicated to you?

RENÉ

Yes, Madame, and I begin to think like you that it is not in the liver as the Greeks and Romans believed, but in convolutions of the brain that the all powerful hand of fate writes its omens.

CATHERINE

You have completed the experiments?

RENÉ

Yes, both of them.

CATHERINE

Tell me all the details.

RENÉ

I obtained two chickens, as you recommended—without a single white blemish.

CATHERINE

That's it—

RENÉ

I lay the first on the little altar and I opened its breast with a single blow of the knife.

CATHERINE

A single one, right? Well?

RENÉ

It let out three shrieks and it expired.

CATHERINE

Three shrieks—three deaths—and then?

RENÉ

The liver twisted to the left, contrary to the usual way.

CATHERINE

Dethronement! Dethronement! Three deaths followed by a dethronement! Do you know this is frightful, René?

RENÉ

Yes, Madame, frightening.

CATHERINE

And the second sacrifice—the one whose brain you must consult?

RENÉ

Frightened by the three cries of the first, when I went to go take it, it flew away—and it extinguished the magic candle which provided light for me.

CATHERINE

You see, René, you see. It's thus our race will be extinguished. Death will touch it with its wing and it will disappear from the earth. Three sons, now—three sons! What did you do next?

RENÉ

I relit the candle and I caught it, cut off its head with a single blow.

CATHERINE

It didn't shriek this time, I hope?

RENÉ

No, but it uttered three sighs.

CATHERINE

You see, René, instead of three shrieks, three sighs, three always, three! They will all three die. All these souls before expiring count and call three times. And then, then what did you do?

RENÉ

In accordance with your instructions, I observed the windings in the brain and in the blood fibers, I observed a letter.

CATHERINE

A letter. A single one?

RENÉ

Yes, but visible—and not to be mistaken.

CATHERINE

And what was this letter?

RENÉ

An 'H'. This 'H' was followed by four perpendicular lines which seemed like the number one repeated four times.

CATHERINE

That's it, that's it. Charles IX reigns—after Charles the IX comes Henry the III, after Henry III, Henry IV—it's him—always him.

RENÉ

But the Duke Francis?

CATHERINE

Doubtless he will be killed in the interval. Oh, Henry IV, Henry IV will reign, René, I am cursed in my posterity.

RENÉ

So—you think he will reign?

CATHERINE

Yes, unless we force the omens to lie.

RENÉ

Your Majesty wishes me to undertake further experiments?

CATHERINE

Tell me, René, isn't there a curious story of a doctor from Perugia, who, condemned to death by the tyrant of Siena for having refused to give him a book dealing with magic, poisoned the book before dying?

RENÉ

Yes, Madame, so well that the tyrant, having seized the book and having read the book without suspecting the venom that it contained, died three days after the victim.

CATHERINE

Tell me, how dies the poison act?

RENÉ

It's very simple, Madame, the leaves of the book, impregnated with a mixture of arsenic stick together. The tyrant in his ignorance pushed them with his finger—and naturally wet his finger to push them with greater ease—several times he put his finger in his mouth and poisoned himself.

CATHERINE

Oh—that's right. I remembered the event but I had forgotten the details. René, I saw at your apartment and asked for a book on hunting—very interesting and very old—did you bring it for me?

RENÉ

Yes, Madame, here it is. It's a book by Pietramonte on the art of raising falcons, male falcons, gyrfalcons.

CATHERINE

Give me this book.

RENÉ

Here it is, Madame.

CATHERINE

Thanks.

RENÉ

Your Majesty has other orders to give me?

CATHERINE

Relative to what?

RENÉ

Relative to this book.

CATHERINE

No, none.

RENÉ

(aside)

She distrusts me.

CATHERINE

Goodbye, René.

RENÉ

(leaving)

Oh, I begin to believe I was wrong to make myself an enemy of the King of Navarre.

(Exit René.)

(Catherine goes to the secret armoire, takes a glass mask, gloves, dips the pages of the book in an antique earthenware vase, re-shuts the armoire and dries the leaves of the book by a chimney fire.)

CATHERINE

I distrust everyone! Even René. So this time, no accomplices—and if he escapes, well, it will truly be a miracle—

(knocking on the door)

Who wants me? I said I wouldn't see anyone except the Duke d'Alençon.

VOICE

(outside the door)

It's he madam.

CATHERINE

Fine, fine, I will open for him myself.

(She puts the book in the armoire, puts out the brazier with water, and puts the mask and gloves on a table and opens the door.)

CATHERINE

(opening the door)

Ah, it's you, my son.

DUKE

Excuse me, Madame, I disturb you.

CATHERINE

No—I was just burning some old parchments and the odor you smell is that of juniper which I am burning to get rid of the other.

DUKE

You had something to ask me, mother?

CATHERINE

Yes, my son—you know that Henry is a greater friend than ever of King Charles?

DUKE

No, I didn't know it, but I suspected it must be so. Now, mother, as my brother-in-law, Little Henry, is a prudent man, he's not reassured.

CATHERINE

So that?

DUKE

So that I think he's preparing everything to flee.

CATHERINE

You believe it, and I am sure of it.

DUKE

Well, mother, what do you think should happen?

CATHERINE

I think he must be allowed to leave.

DUKE

But then, he will escape us, mother.

CATHERINE

He's leaving—but he won't escape us.

DUKE

I don't understand you, mother.

CATHERINE

Listen carefully, Francis—a very able doctor predicted to me yesterday that the King of Navarre was on the point of being killed by one of those diseases which never forgive and for which science knows no remedy—so, you understand, my son, if he must effectively die from such a cruel illness—better that he die far from us, rather than at court under our eyes.

DUKE

Yes, that would cause us too much trouble. But are you sure, Madame, that he is threatened by this illness—and who is the doctor?

CATHERINE

It's the same that predicted the death of his mother—why, not being mistaken about the mother would he be mistaken about the son?

DUKE

Yes, you are right. But if he leaves feeling well—do you think that this illness will take him off while he's on his way?

CATHERINE

No—assuredly, he will leave ill—in all probability. But enough on this subject, my son—and let's talk of other things. Didn't Henry ask you yesterday for a book on hunting? You told me this at least to prove to me to what extent he intends to make his court to King Charles who appreciates in this world God's great hunters.

DUKE

Yes, Madame, I told you that.

CATHERINE

And have you given him the book?

DUKE

Not yet.

CATHERINE

Good! I found at René's, the perfumer's, one of the most curious books on the hunt which exist. There are only two or three copies in the world. I've had this book since this morning. Do you understand, Francis?

DUKE

Yes, I understand.

CATHERINE

(taking the book)

It's a work on the act of raising and dressing falcons, male falcons and gyrfalcons—written by a very wise man for the Lord Castruccio Castracani, the tyrant of Luca—here it is.

DUKE

(looking at the book with a certain terror)

And what am I to do with it, Madame?

CATHERINE

Why take it to your brother, Little Henry, who asked you for it to instruct him in the science of falconry; as he is hunting with falcons today with the King, he won't fail to read a few pages. All you have to do is to be sure to give it to him.

DUKE

Oh—I wouldn't dare go that far, Madame!

CATHERINE

Why's that? It's a book like any other except that it's been shut up for so long that the pages are stuck together. Don't try to read it yourself, Francis, for one cannot begin to read it without wetting one's finger and pushing the pages leaf by leaf—which takes a lot of time and gives much trouble.

DUKE

So much so that only a man who has a great desire to learn would lose the time or take the trouble.

CATHERINE

Exactly, my son and you understand wonderfully.

(The fanfare for the hunt can be heard.)

DUKE

(looking out the window)

Eh! Madame—there exactly is Little Henry in the court—I am going to profit by his absence to take this book to his apartment. On his return he will find it.

CATHERINE

I would prefer that you give it to him, personally, Francis. That would be more sure.

DUKE

I told you that I wouldn't dare go that far.

CATHERINE

Go there, but at least place it in a corner that's very noticeable.

DUKE

Open? Would it be inconvenient if it were open?

CATHERINE

No.

DUKE

Give it to me then, Madame.

CATHERINE

Oh—take it boldly—there's no danger, since I am touching it—besides, you have gloves.

DUKE

Fine, Madame.

CATHERINE

Hurry—Henry is no longer in the court and he might return from one moment to the next.

DUKE

I am going there, Madame.

A PAGE

(entering)

Milord, the King of Navarre, asks, before going on the hunt. the favor of presenting his homage to Your Majesty.

CATHERINE

(to the Duke)

Well, you see, it's God who sends him to you.

(to page)

Tell my son, Henry, that I am not here—but let him enter and wait; his brother-in-law, the Duke of Alençon will keep him company.

DUKE

(hesitating)

Madame—

CATHERINE

Compare the gain with the risk and take courage—Come on.

DUKE

But why not give it to him yourself, Madame?

CATHERINE

Stupid! Do you think he's forgotten his mother's perfumed gloves?

DUKE

That's true.

(Catherine leaves.)

DUKE

Come on, Francis—courage! Yes, she said it, she who knows what it is, the risk—it's only a little audacity—and the gain is a crown.

HENRY

(entering)

Ah, it's you my dear brother—I am always happy to meet you, you know.

DUKE

I came to greet the Queen before my departure for the hunt.

HENRY

By God! That's sympathy—and I too, you see.

DUKE

Brother, in your desire to pay your court to the King, who, before all other types of hunting, prefers falconing, you asked me for a book dealing with this subject.

HENRY

Yes, and you were good enough to tell me that in your library—

DUKE

—was shut up a precious work. That work—here it is.

HENRY

By God! This falls out wonderfully—I will still have time to educate myself before leaving for the hunt. A thousand thanks my very dear brother—and if in my turn, I can be agreeable to you—

DUKE

Rest easy, I will address myself to you. But our good mother is very tardy and I must go to the stables to see about a new horse that I will ride today. Goodbye Henry.

HENRY

We will meet again at the hunt.

DUKE

Certainly.

HENRY

Well—till we meet again.

DUKE

Till we meet again.

(He leaves.)

HENRY

(alone)

Ah, on my word, I am playing lucky. I was waiting for this book with great impatience. Poor Bernese peasant accustomed to hunt bears in our great forests, I am ignorant of the art of falconry— very practical for gentleman of the court. In ten minutes, I will learn how they launch their falcons, I will pursue mine, I will immerse myself in the rules. I will reach the pavilion of Francis the 1st and from there the route of d'Estampes—and may God live, once at Estampes, once in open country, once at the head of fifty cavaliers—I will brave all the Maurevals in the world— and all this I will owe to—The Art of Raising Falcons, Male Falcons and Gyrfalcons. They have forgotten eagles. Well, I will show them how the eagles are raised. But no one is coming—is it that the Queen Mother takes little pleasure in seeing me? I have made my presence known. Should I leave? My word, I am going.

(King Charles enters dressed for the hunt followed by his dog, Acteon.)

THE KING

Ah, it's you, Little Henry? Not yet ready.

HENRY

Sire, I ask a thousand pardons of Your Majesty, but I didn't wish to leave without presenting my respects to our good mother.

THE KING

You are right, Henry—she loves you so much!

HENRY

But you don't need to wait for that, sire; I ask for 10 minutes with Your Majesty and in 10 minutes—

THE KING

Go!

(seeing the book)

But what have you got there? Is it that having married a savant you are becoming a savant, by chance? A book—a book under Little Henry's arm—Miracle! Noel! Hosanna! Little Henry displays his library. By Gog and Magog—this is curious.

HENRY

My word, yes—it's curious. But when Your Majesty learns that it's from devotion to him that I am becoming a philosopher, I hope he won't doubt any more the feelings I've always had for him.

THE KING

How's that? You are becoming a philosopher for me?

HENRY

For you alone, Sire.

THE KING

Explain yourself. You know I love your explanations. They are usually honest and frank.

HENRY

Sire, Your Majesty recalls that he reproached my ignorance in the art of falconry.

THE KING

Yes, I said that ignorance was unworthy of a gentleman.

HENRY

Well, Sire, I've obtained, through my research, a very curious book in which I am going to study the art, so as to be worthy to accompany the King whenever he does me the honor to invite me to the hunt with him.

THE KING

And I will do you this honor often, Henry—for, by God—your company is among those that please me most. And what is this book?

HENRY

Sire, it's a tract on the art of raising falcons dedicated to Lord Castruccio Castracani, Tyrant of Lucca.

THE KING

By God! By Pietramonte?

HENRY

My word, yes, Your Majesty knows this book?

THE KING

I've been searching for it for ten years and I searched in vain.
There exist only three copies in the world. Give me this book,
Henry.

HENRY

Oh! Sire, with great pleasure.

THE KING

And where the devil did you find it?

HENRY

By God—in your very family. And it's true, as they say one
sometimes searches for what is very near. Your brother,
d'Alençon just gave it to me.

THE KING

My brother d'Alençon? You see the snake! Go dress, Henry, go
dress. For today, again I overlook your ignorance.

HENRY

Where does Your Majesty order me to rejoin him?

THE KING

In the court of the Louvre, where I will be after I've had a word with my mother.

HENRY

Sire, at Your Majesty's orders.

(Henry exits.)

THE KING

d'Alençon had this book and never mentioned it to me. I no longer wonder he's such a clever falconer and that he knows everything concerning the nourishment and education of birds.

(sitting and opening the book)

It doesn't seem to have been much used. The leaves are stuck together.

(trying to open them)

Well—

(wetting a finger and forcing the page to turn)

That's it.

(reading)

They must be nourished, as soon as they begin to get their feathers with the hearts of brave and valiant animals.

DUKE

(having entered the room)

He's still here—he's reading.

THE KING

(wetting his finger)

"Brave and valiant—like bulls, bears and wolves."

DUKE

(aside)

Mercy! It's not him—it's my brother.

(making a motion to stop the King)

Well, what am I going to do? It's still the same risk—only instead of the crown of Navarre, it's the crown of France—read on, dear brother, read on!

THE KING

(reading)

"Then when they begin to fly—when they begin to fly, it's a question of introducing living birds into their cages, and to make sure they don't eat the brains of which they are very fond. It is necessary, amongst the smaller birds to choose the most courageous such as goldfinches, chaffinches and French spar-rows and not turtledoves, nightingales and warblers." Cursed leaves, turn. Ah, it's you d'Alençon?

DUKE

Yes, Milord.

THE KING

What, have you such treasures in your library and you never told me?

DUKE

But I myself ask Your Majesty how this book found its way into your hands?

THE KING

It's the simplest thing, I met Henry here; Henry brought this book with him. I had been ashamed to leave such a pearl with a bore like him. I took it from his hands—and I was reading it when you arrived. But you came for something?

DUKE

Yes, sire, only I am in a position to tell you what brought me.

THE KING

Fine, some new rumor, some daily accusation against poor Little Henry.

DUKE

Exactly.

THE KING

It's the tenth one this month—but never mind—come with me and you will tell me about it—Ah—!

DUKE

What's wrong, sire?

THE KING

I don't know—a cold sweat. My knees shake. Some air, I am suffocating.

DUKE

The weather is bad and doubtless.

THE KING

What are you saying, d'Alençon? The heaven is like an azure. Oh—what is it, what can it be?

(He lets the book fall, the dog picks it up.)

DUKE

Your Majesty.

THE KING

I'm better. It's nothing—come, d'Alençon, come!

DUKE

(aside, following him)

He's tasted ten times the poison—he's dead.

CURTAIN

ACT III

SCENE 9

The forest of Saint Germain. On one side a clearing shaded by a great oak tree. On the other, the pavilion of Francis I.

LA MÔLE

It seemed to me that the hunt was singularly near us just now. I heard cries of huntsmen encouraging the falcons.

COCONNAS

And now, nothing more can be heard. Therefore, they must be further off. I told you it was a bad place for observation—true we can't be seen—but, we can't see much either.

LA MÔLE

What the devil, my dear Hannibal, it's better to put our horses some place rather than lead them like two mules carrying baggage so that I don't know how they will be able to follow us—well, I only know these old beech trees and oaks which can take on this work. I dare say that far from blaming de Mouy, I recognize in all the preparation of this enterprise the mind of a true conspirator.

COCONNAS

Good—the word escaped you now. We are conspiring then. Ah, I've got you now.

LA MÔLE

The word did not escape me, Coconnas—I said by design—yes, we are conspiring—if to help a king and queen to flee is to conspire.

COCONNAS

Who are conspiring! It's known, in every country in the world as being accomplices to a conspiracy and to be accomplices to a conspiracy is to conspire. You cannot get out of that dilemma, my poor La Môle, logician though you are.

LA MÔLE

Coconnas, I told you, I repeat to you, I am not forcing you in any way to aid me in this adventure—to which I am led by a particular sentiment you do not share and cannot share.

COCONNAS

Eh! By God! Who pretends that you are forcing me? First of all, I know of no man who can force Coconnas to do what he does not wish to do. But do you think I will let you without following you, especially when I see you are going to the devil?

LA MÔLE

Hannibal, Hannibal. I think that I see down there her white saddle mare. Oh—it's strange that only thinking of her coming, my heart beats.

COCONNAS

Well, mine doesn't beat at all—it's funny.

LA MÔLE

It's not she—I was deceived. What's happening then? It seems to me it was for four o'clock.

COCONNAS

What's happened is that it's not yet four o'clock—and we still have time to take a nap it appears. Let's take a nap.

LA MÔLE

Hannibal, I repeat—Hannibal, I beg you—don't stay here an instant longer—you are the servant of Madame de Nevers, as I am of the Queen—well Madame de Nevers is not coming with us.

COCONNAS

Ah, exactly—there's the difference between the two of us, La Môle and what makes me better or worse than you—let the moralists decide—I prefer my friend to my mistress while you prefer your mistress to your friend.

LA MÔLE

Oh, Coconnas, it's not love I have for Madame Marguerite, it's delirium, madness, religion—I prefer to die for her than to live without her. I think of her incessantly, I think of her during the day, during the night, while I wake, when I sleep.

COCONNAS

Well—when I sleep, I think of nothing—so to think of nothing
I am going to sleep. Good day La Môle—when the hour comes
to act, awaken me.

(He lies down, but the moment he puts his head on the ground
he stops.)

COCONNAS

Oh—oh!

LA MÔLE

What's wrong?

COCONNAS

This time I am not mistaken—I hear something.

LA MÔLE

That's strange, I have good hearing—I hear nothing.

COCONNAS

You don't hear anything?

LA MÔLE

No.

COCONNAS

Well—look at this deer.

LA MÔLE

Where?

COCONNAS

Down there.

LA MÔLE

He's eating.

COCONNAS

He's listening.

LA MÔLE

I think you are right, for now he's running away.

COCONNAS

Then since he's fleeing, it's because he hears what you do not.

LA MÔLE

In fact, the galloping of a horse. Attention. Attention.

(Marguerite on a white horse passes in the depth of the stage at a gallop, making a sign.)

LA MÔLE

The Queen! The Queen!

COCONNAS

What's it mean? She passed by and made a sign that's all.

LA MÔLE

The sign means, "I will be with you right away."

COCONNAS

The sign meant "Leave, it is time."

LA MÔLE

The gesture signified—"Wait for me."

COCONNAS

The gesture signifies "Escape."

LA MÔLE

Well, let's each act according to his conviction. You go—I'll stay.

COCONNAS

Simpleton!

(He sits back down.)

LA MÔLE

De Mouy—de Mouy fleeing!

COCONNAS

You see we must escape since de Mouy is in flight.

DE MOUY

(passing at a gallop)

Eh! Hurry! Hurry! All is lost! En route! En route! Those who came here for Monsieur d'Alençon, en route!

LA MÔLE

And the Queen! The Queen!

(De Mouy disappears without responding.)

COCONNAS

(running to his horse)

My friend, I repeat what de Mouy said, for de Mouy is a man who speaks well. By God, as King Charles says—when one conspires badly, you must escape well—my horse.

(a squire leads in the horse)

In saddle, La Môle, in saddle.

LA MÔLE

Well, look, to horse since you wish it, but to search for her at least?

COCONNAS

(on his horse)

This is very fortunate.

A LIEUTENANT

Halt there, gentleman.

(From the trees appears a company of light cavalry.)

COCONNAS

What did I tell you?

LA MÔLE

Ah!

COCONNAS

Nothing is yet lost—listen and imitate me.

(to the light cavalry)

One moment, one moment, gentleman. What's wrong?

LIEUTENANT

You must surrender.

COCONNAS

(dismounting)

Gentleman—we surrender.

(they are surrounded)

But first of all—why must we surrender?

LIEUTENANT

You may ask the King of Navarre.

COCONNAS

What crime have we committed?

LIEUTENANT

Monsieur d'Alençon will tell you. Gentleman, the King.

THE KING

(with the Duke and their suite)

Come on, come on, I am in haste to return to the Louvre. You say our heretics are in this pavilion.

DUKE

Yes, sire.

THE KING

Come on, come on! Let us drag them from the earth. Let us pitch them to the hounds. Today's Saint Blaise day—cousin to St. Bartholomew.

DUKE

Open the gates.

(A door opens and a group of Huguenots come out.)

THE KING

Very fine—I see some Huguenots. I don't say the contrary but I don't see either Henry or Marguerite. You promised them to me, d'Alençon.

DUKE

Then, sire, it's because they've fled.

MADAME DE NEVERS

Fled? Not at all, sire, for here they come.

THE KING

And come like two lovers—here, Little Henry—here.

(Henry and Marguerite enter.)

HENRY

Your Majesty calls me?

THE KING

Yes.

HENRY

Here I am, at your orders, Sire!

THE KING

(to Marguerite)

And you?

MARGUERITE

Me, too, brother.

THE KING

Where are you coming from, sir?

HENRY

From the hunt, Sire!

THE KING

The hunt was on the banks of the river—and not in the forest and Monsieur d'Alençon saw you both spur for the forest.

HENRY

My falcon was after a pheasant and as I am a bad huntsman with falcons—seeing I couldn't call him back—I followed him.

(aside)

Ah! You saw us—! Wait!

THE KING

And where is this pheasant.

THE KING

Here it is, sire—a magnificent cock.

THE KING

Why didn't you rejoin us after this pheasant was taken?

HENRY

Because at the moment, for rejoining you, Sire, we saw Your Majesty coming this way—then we took to galloping in your traces being on the hunt with Your Majesty. We didn't wish to lose you.

THE KING

(pointing to the Huguenots)

And all these gentlemen were part of my hunt?

HENRY

What gentlemen?

THE KING

Eh! Your Huguenots, by God! In any event, if someone invited them, It wasn't me.

HENRY

No, sire, but perhaps it was Monsieur d'Alençon.

DUKE

Me?

HENRY

Doubtless—wasn't there something between de Mouy and you—like a promise on your part to accept the throne of Navarre—which I had renounced?

THE KING

To accept the throne of Navarre? You were accepting the throne of Navarre, d'Alençon?

DUKE

Sire!

HENRY

Ask of all these gentlemen? Why were you here, gentlemen? I ask you on your honor. Was it for the Duke d'Alençon?

A HUGUENOT

It wasn't for you, since you had refused the throne de Mouy proposed you.

HENRY

You hear, sire?

THE KING

Is this the truth, gentlemen?

ALL

Yes, sire, it's the truth.

THE KING

You were here for the Duke d'Alençon?

HUGUENOT

Yes, sire. Monsieur d'Alençon had to flee and we were to provide him an escort.

DUKE

They are lying! They are lying!

THE KING

Ah—I wish now, once in my life to know what to believe.

HENRY

De Mouy—is he among the prisoners? Sire, call de Mouy—he will tell you that this flight was arranged with Monsieur d'Alençon—that yesterday he came to offer me to partake in it.

THE KING

Where is de Mouy—is de Mouy among the prisoners?

DE NANCY

No, sire, he escaped, or so it appears.

THE KING

(noticing La Môle and Coconnas)

But here are two other prisoners—let's question them. Come here, gentlemen.

(Coconnas and La Môle approach. La Môle bows, Coconnas salutes in the grand manner)

To whom do you belong, gentlemen?

COCONNAS

We belong to ourselves, Sire.

THE KING

You don't belong to anyone?

COCONNAS

No, Sire.

THE KING

What were you doing when they arrested you?

COCONNAS

We were devising feats of arms and love.

THE KING

On horseback, armed to the teeth, ready to flee?

COCONNAS

Pardon, sire, Your Majesty is ill informed—we were sleeping under the shade of an oak—sub tegmini fugi, as my friend de La Môle says.

THE KING

What did you see?

COCONNAS

We saw some people fleeing.

THE KING

What did you hear?

COCONNAS

We heard de Mouy who shouted "All is lost—en route, those who belong to Monsieur d'Alençon, en route."

THE KING

He shouted that?

COCONNAS

Sire, Your Majesty does not suppose that a gentleman can lie?

THE KING

And despite this warning, you didn't flee?

COCONNAS

We had no reason to flee, sire. We are not with Monsieur d'Alençon.

DUKE

They did not flee because their horses were far way.

COCONNAS

I beg Your Majesty's pardon, Milord. We were holding our horses by the bridal—and in fact, I was already on horseback when these gentlemen appeared, and then I dismounted. Isn't it true, gentlemen, that we could flee, and that we did not wish to?

LIEUTENANT

It's true.

MADAME DE NEVERS

Dear Hannibal—go on! How I love you!

DUKE

But these pack horses, these mules, and these loaded trunks?

COCONNAS

That is not our concern at all, Milord. Are we stable valets? Search the groom who was guarding them and he will answer.

DUKE

(furious)

The groom has disappeared.

COCONNAS

Then it's because he got frightened. What do you expect, Milord, you cannot expect a serf to have the calm of a gentleman.

THE KING

Well, well—we shall look into all this. Henry, your word not to flee.

HENRY

I give it, Sire.

THE KING

Return to Paris—and take the prisoners to your room. Your swords, gentleman.

(Coconnas and La Môle surrender their swords)

THE KING

Now, let's leave.

(He staggers.)

MARGUERITE

What's wrong with you, brother? What pain do you feel? This is the second time since the beginning of the hunt.

THE KING

Oh, I feel—I feel what Portia must have felt when she swallowed burning coals. My horse! My horse!

HENRY

(to Marguerite)

What's wrong with him again?

MARGUERITE

I don't know—but nothing good, surely.

THE KING

My legs shake—I cannot see. mercy! I am burning—I am burning! Help me, gentlemen, help me!

HENRY

The King feels unwell, gentlemen—a stretcher, a litter to take the King back to Paris.

MARGUERITE

Well, brother?

THE KING

It's getting a little better. To Paris, gentlemen, to Paris.

(The suite of the King goes off crossing the forest.)

MARGUERITE

(to La Môle as she leaves)

Me deide!

COCONNAS

What did she say to you?

LA MÔLE

Two words in Greek—meaning "fear nothing."

COCONNAS

So much the worse, La Môle, so much the worse. That bodes us no good. Every time that word has been said to me in the way of encouragement, I have received, almost at the same moment—either a gunshot wound, or a sword cut to the body or a pot of flowers on my head—fear nothing—be it in Greek, Latin or French has always meant to me—"Watch out below".

LIEUTENANT

En route, gentlemen.

COCONNAS

And where are we being taken, if you please?

LIEUTENANT

To Vincennes, I think.

COCONNAS

I would much prefer to go elsewhere but one cannot always go where one wishes. Let's go, La Môle.

CURTAIN

ACT IV
SCENE 10

The King's Arms Room—the Louvre.

The King, supported by a captain of the Guard, sits on some cushions accompanied by de Nancey.

THE KING

Let someone inform Master Ambrose Paré that I have become indisposed during the hunt, and that I order him instantly to the Louvre. Then tell Henry that I wish to speak to him.

(They leave. He collapses on the cushions. Henry enters.)

HENRY

Sire, you asked for me.

THE KING

(giving him his hand and gesturing with his head)

Yes.

HENRY

(refusing his hand)

Sire, you are forgetting that I am not your brother, but your prisoner.

THE KING

That's true. But I recall that while the litter was being brought up, when we were alone, you promised me to answer frankly my questions.

HENRY

I am ready to keep that promise. Question me, Sire.

THE KING

(pouring cold water on his hand and putting his hand over his face)

Was there any truth in the accusations of the Duke d'Alençon—speak.

HENRY

Entirely, if he accuses me of only wishing to flee.

THE KING

You admit that you wish to flee?

HENRY

As far away as I could possibly get.

THE KING

And why flee? Are you unhappy with me, Henry?

HENRY

No, sire, and God, who can read in my heart, sees, on the contrary what a profound affection I bear to my brother and King—anyway, it is neither my brother nor my King that I would flee.

THE KING

And who would you flee then?

HENRY

I would flee those who detest me—Your Majesty permits me to speak to him here with an open heart?

THE KING

Speak—who detests you here?

HENRY

Those who detest me here—Monsieur d'Alençon and the Queen Mother.

THE KING

And you think this hate—?

HENRY

Is a mortal hate; yes, I believe it.

THE KING

The proof!

HENRY

Let Your Majesty recall St. Bartholomew—which I only escaped by a miracle.

THE KING

Yes, yes, Little Henry—you speak true. And you think those who wish you ill are not stopped by seeing that I do not wish you any harm.

HENRY

Sire, I am astonished every evening to find myself among the living!

THE KING

(with melancholy)

It's because, at bottom, they know I love you, Henry—that they wish to kill you—but be easy, they will be punished for this ill will—I am watching over you Henry, and misfortune to those who renew such attempts! Henry, you are free!

HENRY

Free to leave Paris, sire?

THE KING

Not at all. You know indeed that it is impossible for me to let you go. Look, Henry, I repeat, I have affection for you—whatever they can say and do, whatever I have said and done, I want you to stay, for I want to have someone who loves me—and God pardon me, I think in this world there is only you and Acteon.

(looking)

Where the devil is Acteon! Give me a glass of water, Henry—I am burning.

HENRY

Well, sire, if Your Majesty protects me from her, I will pray him to grant me a grace.

(He gives a glass to the King.)

THE KING

(taking the glass)

Which? Go on! I am listening.

(drinking)

HENRY

It's to keep me near him not with the title of friend, but as a prisoner.

THE KING

(after having emptied his glass)

What do you mean a prisoner?

HENRY

(taking back the glass)

Doubtless! Doesn't Your Majesty see that it is your friendship which is destroying me?

THE KING

And you prefer my hate?

HENRY

An open hate—yes, Sire, for this hate will save me. So long as I am believed in disgrace with Your Majesty, there will be less rush to see me dead.

THE KING

I don't know what you want—Little Henry. I don't know what your end is, but if your wishes are not accomplished, if you fail in your goal, I will be much surprised.

HENRY

I can then count on the severity of the King?

THE KING

Yes.

HENRY

Well, in that case, Sire, recommend me to the Captain of your guards as a man that your rage gives only a week to live. That way I will love you a long while.

THE KING

Monsieur de Nancey.

(The Captain of the guards enters.)

THE KING

Monsieur de Nancy, I place the most guilty man in the realm in your hands. You will answer to me on your head.

(low)

Is that it, Little Henry?

HENRY

(low)

Thanks, Sire.

(He bows humbly and leaves with de Nancey.)

THE KING

(alone)

He's right, a hundred times right—but what the devil has become of my dog. Hola Acteon—hola! Come here, come—ah, what's wrong with him then

(finds the dog)

Dead—rigid, cold and sleeping on a cloak of mine. Poor beast! He would have wanted to die on this object which recalls a friend to him. Dead! But dead of what? This morning he was marvelously healthy. He followed me to my mother's, he came back here carrying my book. Let's see then.

(kneeling before the dog)

His eye is watery, tongue red—oh! This is a strange illness. What's he still got in his mouth? Some paper. Near this paper the most violent swelling—the flesh is corroded as if by vitroil.

(unfolding some of the paper)

What is this? A fragment of my book on hunting, by chance, was the book poisoned? A thousand demons! And I touched each page with my finger and at each page put my finger in my mouth to wet it. This dizziness, this aching, this vomiting—I am dead! Monsieur de Nancey! Monsieur de Nancey!

(Monsieur de Nancey.)

THE KING

Let someone rush instantly to the Pont Saint Michel. Let them bring Master René the Florentine, you hear! Willingly or by force, let him be brought. He must be here in ten minutes.

DE NANCY

Sire, this falls out wonderfully, he just went into the Queen Mother's apartments.

THE KING

Have him take his leave and bring him here.

(Monsieur de Nancey leaves)

Oh, if I have to torture the whole world, I will know where this book came from.

DE NANCY

(returning)

Here's Master René, Sire, I met him in the corridor.

THE KING

Bring him in.

(René enters.)

THE KING

Enter! Enter! Shut the door on us, Monsieur de Nancey.

(Monsieur de Nancey exits.)

RENÉ

(trembling)

Your Majesty has something to ask of me?

THE KING

Yes, you are an adept chemist, right?

RENÉ

Sire!

THE KING

And you know more about certain subjects than the cleverest doctors?

RENÉ

Your Majesty exaggerates.

THE KING

No, my mother told me. Besides, I have confidence in you—and I always preferred to consult you than any other. Here, look at the body of this dog and tell me what killed him.

RENÉ

(examining the jaws of the dog)

These are very sad symptoms, Sire.

THE KING

Yes, the dog died poisoned, right?

RENÉ

I fear so.

THE KING

And can you say with certainty that he was poisoned?

RENÉ

There's no doubt about it, I am sure of it. See this redness, sire, these pustules. I can almost tell what poison was given to him.

THE KING

What poison?

RENÉ

A mineral poison, according to all probability.

THE KING

Oh! And what would happen to a man who had, inadvertently, swallowed some of this same poison?

RENÉ

A great dizziness of the head, burning insides, aches in the bowels, vomiting.

THE KING

That's indeed it—and would he be thirsty?

RENÉ

An inextinguishable thirst.

THE KING

That's indeed it! That's indeed it—

(He pours a glass of water and drinks.)

RENÉ

What is the purpose of all these questions, Sire?

THE KING

Little matter to me! Reply to me, that's all. And what is the antidote?

RENÉ

You must first all be sure—

THE KING

You said it was a mineral poison?

RENÉ

Yes, but there are several mineral poisons—does Your Majesty have some idea of the way this dog was poisoned?

THE KING

He ate a page of a book.

RENÉ

Of a book?

THE KING

Yes.

RENÉ

And Your Majesty has this book?

THE KING

Here it is!

(Showing the book to René.)

RENÉ

(recoiling)

My God.

THE KING

Ah—wait—here it is!

(points to a half-torn page)

RENÉ

Let me tear out another, sire.

THE KING

The same—the same—it will be better.

(tearing out what is left of the page and giving it to René)

RENÉ

(puts the page to a candle and burns it)

It has been poisoned with a mixture of arsenic.

THE KING

How can you tell that?

RENÉ

From the odor of this page.

THE KING

Are you sure of it?

RENÉ

As I had myself prepared the mixture.

THE KING

And the antidote?

(René shakes his head.)

THE KING

What? You don't know one?

RENÉ

Sire, it's a terrible poison.

THE KING

It doesn't kill right away?

RENÉ

No, but it kills surely—little matter the time one takes to die.

THE KING

Since one is surely dying, right? It's almost a calculation, I know. Now, you know this book?

RENÉ

Me?

THE KING

You know it. Just now, seeing it, you started back in horror.

RENÉ

Sire, I swear to you—

THE KING

René, listen carefully—you poisoned the Queen of Navarre with gloves; you poisoned the Prince of Porcian with fumes from a lamp—you attempted to poison de Condé with a scented apple. René, I will tear your flesh off piece by piece with a burning pincers if you don't tell me to whom this book belonged.

RENÉ

And if I tell the truth, who will guarantee me that I won't be punished more cruelly than if I keep silent?

THE KING

I....

RENÉ

You will give me your royal word?

THE KING

Word of a gentleman—you will escape with your life.

RENÉ

Sire, this book belonged to me.

THE KING

To you?

RENÉ

Yes, to me.

THE KING

And how did it leave your hands?

RENÉ

The Queen Mother obtained it from me.

THE KING

And when she obtained it, was it poisoned?

RENÉ

No.

THE KING

But for what purpose did she obtain it? You must know.

RENÉ

For the purpose of giving it to the King of Navarre who had asked the Duke d'Alençon for a book of this type to study falconry.

THE KING

Oh—that's it. I understand everything. I have it all, now—this book was put in the hands of Henry—there was fate in it—and I submit to it.

(uttering several screams of pain, he falls on his cushions)

RENÉ

What's wrong with you, Sire?

THE KING

Nothing! Only give me something to drink, René. I am burning!

RENÉ

Oh! My God! My God! What's happened then?

THE KING

Now take this pen—and write on this book.

RENÉ

What must I write?

THE KING

What I am going to dictate to you. "This hunting manual was given by me to the Queen Mother, Catherine de Medici"— signed, René.

RENÉ

You promised to save my life.

THE KING

And I will maintain my word, but—

(putting his finger to his lips)

RENÉ

Oh, sire, there is nothing more sacred.

THE KING

Now, there is no antidote, you said—but still you won't let your father or your brother die, if they had been poisoned like this dog—without giving them something—what would you give them?

(René bows without responding.)

RENÉ

(with despair)

Nothing!

DE NANCY

Sire, the Queen Mother.

THE KING

She mustn't see you here—through this corridor—go!

(pointing the way to an exit that he urges René to use)

Ah, the Queen Mother—I am curious to know what she's come to tell me. Let's hide this book.

(He hides the book.)

CATHERINE

(entering)

I learned, my son, that you were indisposed on your return from the hunt.

THE KING

They misinformed you, Madame—I've been sick since this morning.

CATHERINE

And I think I bring to Your Majesty the remedy which ought to cure your body and soul.

THE KING

(low)

A thousand devils! Does she find I am not dying fast enough?

(aloud)

What is this remedy, Madame? I admit that at this moment, I am in great need.

CATHERINE

It's in the illness itself.

THE KING

And where in the illness?

CATHERINE

Listen, my son. Have you heard sometimes that it is secret enemies whose hate or ambition kills from a distance?

THE KING

By steel or—by poison, Madame?

CATHERINE

No, by ways much more certain; much more terrible.

THE KING

Explain yourself.

CATHERINE

Have you had time to practice the Cabala and magic?

THE KING

(laughing)

Much!

CATHERINE

Well, that's where your sufferings come from—an enemy of Your Majesty who wouldn't dare to attack you openly—has conspired in the shadows. Do you understand of whom I speak?

THE KING

My word, no, Madame.

CATHERINE

Search carefully, and recall certain plans for escape which would assure the murderer's impunity.

THE KING

The murderer, you say? Someone has tried to kill me, mother?

CATHERINE

Yes, my son—you suspect, perhaps, but I—I have become

certain.

THE KING

I never doubt what you tell me, Madame. And how did he try to kill me, Madame? Let's see!

CATHERINE

(pulling a small wax figure from under her cape)

Here!

THE KING

What is this little statuette, Madame?

CATHERINE

You see what it has on it head?

THE KING

A royal crown.

CATHERINE

On the shoulders?

THE KING

A royal cape.

CATHERINE

And in the heart?

THE KING

A needle!

CATHERINE

Well, sire, do you recognize yourself?

THE KING

Me?

CATHERINE

Yes, you have your cape and your crown.

THE KING

Well?

CATHERINE

Well, sire, this figurine was found during the hunt—at the lodge—

THE KING

Of the King of Navarre?

CATHERINE

No, but of de La Môle, his instrument.

THE KING

Ah, this doll was found in the lodge of de La Môle?

CATHERINE

You see what letter is written on the label which bears this needle?

THE KING

An 'M'?

CATHERINE

That means death, Sire, it's the magic formula—the maker writes his vow on the wound he inflicts.

THE KING

So, in your opinion, it's de La Môle who wants to end my days?

CATHERINE

Yes, as the knife that plunges in the heart but behind the dagger—is the arm that directs it.

THE KING

Well, yes, that's the cause—I recognize it, mother—but now, what to do? Speak—I am very ignorant of magic.

CATHERINE

The death of the maker breaks the charm. Let the guilty one die and the charm will cease to work.

THE KING

You are sure of what you are proposing, Madame?

CATHERINE

I am very certain.

THE KING

Well, now I know who to punish, all will go well.

CATHERINE

Yes, provided you punish.

THE KING

See how things fall out, mother, La Môle has already been arrested.

CATHERINE

I said that La Môle was the instrument—only the instrument—you understand?

THE KING

Well, we will begin with de La Môle, mother. All these crises of which I am struck can give birth to dangerous suspicions around us. Perhaps bad people will say I am poisoned.

CATHERINE

Oh!

THE KING

They indeed said that of my brother, Francis II—it is then urgent, as you say, that light be shed on it—and that the brightness of this light reveal the truth.

CATHERINE

So, La Môle—

THE KING

Seems an admirable suspect to me, Madame. Let's start with him at first, and if as you say, the King of Navarre is his accomplice—he will speak.

CATHERINE

(low)

Yes, and if he doesn't speak, they will make him speak.

(aloud)

Sire, you permit the investigation to begin?

THE KING

Certainly—I wish it, Madame, and the sooner the better.

CATHERINE

My son, you will remember that it was I who—

THE KING

I never forget anything, Madame, rest assured—

MARGUERITE

(raising the door curtain, in a low voice)

Charles! Charles!

CATHERINE

Till we meet again, my son. Then you give me full power to pursue this affair?

THE KING

I give it to you, Madam—and with a full heart.

(Catherine leaves. Marguerite enters.)

MARGUERITE

(rushing towards the King)

Ah, sire, you know very well she's lying, right?

THE KING

Who—mother?

MARGUERITE

Listen, Charles, it's terrible to accuse one's mother, but I suspected that she just came to you to pursue them further and I followed her—oh! On my life, on yours, on our twin soul, I tell you she is lying.

THE KING

Pursuing them? Who is she pursuing?

MARGUERITE

Henry—your Little Henry first of all, who loves you and who is devoted to you more than anyone else in the world.

THE KING

You think so, Marguerite?

MARGUERITE

Oh! Sire, I am sure of it.

THE KING

Well, me, too.

MARGUERITE

Well, if you are sure of it, brother, why have you had him arrested and taken to Vincennes?

THE KING

Because he asked me to, himself.

MARGUERITE

He asked you to do it?

THE KING

Yes, he has singular ideas, Henry and one of these ideas is that he is in greater safety in disgrace than in my favor.

MARGUERITE

Oh, I just understand—and he is in security then?

THE KING

Yes.

MARGUERITE

Thanks, brother; so much for Henry—but—

THE KING

But what?

MARGUERITE

There is another person in whom I am perhaps wrong to interest myself, perhaps, but I am interested in him.

THE KING

And who is this person?

MARGUERITE

Sire, spare me. I hardly dare name him to my brother—and I don't dare to name him to my king.

THE KING

La Môle, right?

MARGUERITE

Sire, he is not guilty, I swear to you.

THE KING

Didn't you understand what our good mother said, poor Margot?

MARGUERITE

Oh! I already begged you not to believe it, brother. I already swore that she is lying.

THE KING

But perhaps you don't know that a wax figure was found by de La Môle.

MARGUERITE

In fact, brother, I know it.

THE KING

That this figure is pierced through the heart by a needle, and that the needle which wounds it has a little barrier and an "M" on it.

MARGUERITE

I know that, too.

THE KING

That this doll has a royal cape on its shoulders and a royal crown on its head.

MARGUERITE

I know all this.

THE KING

Well, what do you say to that?

MARGUERITE

I say that his little doll represents a woman, not a man.

THE KING

And the needle which pierces the heart?

MARGUERITE

It was charm to make the woman fall in love and not a spell to harm a man.

THE KING

And this letter 'M'?

MARGUERITE

It doesn't mean 'mort' or death as the Queen Mother said—it means—oh, brother, pardon me.

(she falls to her knees)

It means Marguerite.

THE KING

Silence, sister! For even if you have understood—you could be understood in your turn.

MARGUERITE

(raising her head)

Oh—what do I care! And is the whole world here to hear me? Before the entire world, I will declare that it is infamous to abuse the love of a gentleman—to soil his reputation with a suspicion of murder.

THE KING

Margot—suppose I told you that I know as well as you who is and who is not guilty?

MARGUERITE

Brother!

THE KING

Suppose I told you de La Môle is innocent?

MARGUERITE

You know it?

THE KING

Suppose I told you that I know who is really guilty?

MARGUERITE

Great God! Who really is guilty? But has a crime really been committed?

THE KING

Voluntarily or involuntarily—yes. There has been a crime committed.

MARGUERITE

Against you?

THE KING

Against me.

MARGUERITE

Oh—no—it can't be.

THE KING

Look at me, Marguerite.

MARGUERITE

Why so pale, brother?

THE KING

Because I don't have a week to live.

MARGUERITE

You, brother? You, my Charles.

(pulling him in her arms)

THE KING

Marguerite, I've been poisoned.

MARGUERITE

Oh—and you know who's guilty?

THE KING

I know.

MARGUERITE

It's not Henry, nor de La Môle, you said that. Could it be? Oh! My God, my voice chokes in my throat—my tongue refuses to say his name—could it be Monsieur d'Alençon?

THE KING

Perhaps.

MARGUERITE

Or indeed—or indeed—could it be?

(lowering her head)

Could it be our mother? Oh my God! My God! This is impossible.

THE KING

Impossible! It's too bad René isn't here—he would tell you my story.

MARGUERITE

Him, René?

THE KING

Yes—he could tell you, for example, that a woman he dared not refuse asked him for a book secreted in his library. That a subtle poison was poured on each page of this book—that this poison destined for someone, I don't know who, fell by a caprice of fate or by a punishment from heaven on a person other than the one for whom it was destined. But in the absence of René, sister, here is this book. You can see written in the hand of the Florentine on the first page of the book—which contained in its pages the death of twenty people, you can see that this book was given by him to our mother.

MARGUERITE

Oh—in your turn, silence, Charles. Silence!

THE KING

You see clearly then how important it is that people believe I am dying from sorcery.

MARGUERITE

But this is sinful! It's frightful! Grace! Mercy, brother—you know very well he is innocent.

THE KING

Yes, I know it—but it's necessary that I believe him guilty. Let your lover die to save the honor of the House of France. I am dying for the same cause—and without complaint, you see.

MARGUERITE

Ah, my brother! But still—if you are mistaken—if you are not going to die.

THE KING

I think I told you that the poison was prepared by our mother. Come, give me your arm, Marguerite, I want to get back to my room.

NURSE

(entering excitedly)

What's the matter with you, my Charles? You are pale—hardly able to stand up. Oh! My God! My God! Madame, what has happened?

THE KING

I'm hot and then cold. You understand that makes me ill. You will watch my door and see no one enters, you understand, nurse—no one!

NURSE

But, if Master Ambrose Paré comes? You sent for him, they told me.

THE KING

You will tell him I am recovering—and that I have no need of a doctor. By the way, this poor Acteon is dead. He must be buried in some corner of the Louvre. He was one of my best friends. I will build a tomb for him—if I have time.

THE KING

Goodbye sister.

(He leaves with the nurse.)

MARGUERITE

Now, La Môle—for you—everything for you.

(She leaves.)

CURTAIN

ACT IV
SCENE 11

A cell in the dungeon of Vincennes. In the rear a large door with a peek-a-boo doors to the right and left.

COCONNAS

(alone and striking the wall)

Say, jailor, my friend, you're frying pan is very warm and I'm suffocating in here. What the devil, if Monsieur d'Alençon has insisted that we be roasted put us on the skewer and be done with it. But if he doesn't exact that, open by God—or I will break the door down.

JAILOR

(entering)

Silence!

COCONNAS

What! You don't want me to yell when I burn? Come on. Am I supposed to be Saint Laurene?

JAILOR

The governor follows me.

COCONNAS

The governor? And what's he here to do?

JAILOR

To visit you.

COCONNAS

He's doing me too much honor. Welcome governor.

(The governor enters with guards from the rear.)

GOVERNOR

(entering, low to the jailor)

Bring the other prisoner here.

(to Coconnas)

Have you any money, sir?

COCONNAS

Me?

GOVERNOR

Yes, you.

COCONNAS

I have three crowns.

GOVERNOR

Some jewels?

COCONNAS

I have a bag.

GOVERNOR

Will you permit me to search you?

COCONNAS

Let you search me?

GOVERNOR

Yes.

COCONNAS

What kind of proposition is that to make a gentleman? By God, sir, it's indeed lucky for you that we are both in prison.

GOVERNOR

Sir, I am in the King's service.

COCONNAS

Tell me, Mr. Governor, the honest people who plunder on the

Saint Michael Bridge. They too are in the service of the King? I didn't know that, and I make them my excuses, up till now I had taken them for thieves.

GOVERNOR

(after having searched Coconnas)

Sir, I salute you.

(La Môle enters by the side door.)

GOVERNOR

It's your turn La Môle.

LA MÔLE

Sir, it's useless for you to search me—I am going to give you all I have on me.

GOVERNOR

What have you?

LA MÔLE

Eighty crowns in this purse.

GOVERNOR

Let me have it. Is that all?

LA MÔLE

Then these jewels—this ring.

GOVERNOR

Fine. Have you anything more?

LA MÔLE

No, sir, on my word.

GOVERNOR

And this chain you wear around your neck.

LA MÔLE

It supports a medallion, sir.

GOVERNOR

Give it to me.

LA MÔLE

A medallion, without any value, I swear.

GOVERNOR

No matter.

LA MÔLE

What? You insist?

GOVERNOR

I have orders not to leave you anything except your clothes and
a medallion is not clothes.

LA MÔLE

Very well, sir, you shall have what you ask for.

(He detaches the medallion, carries to his lips, lets it fall and breaks it with the heel of his boot. He then gives the gold chain to the Governor.

GOVERNOR

Sir!

COCONNAS

Bravo, La Môle.

GOVERNOR

Sir, I shall complain to the King.

(to turnkey)

Escort the prisoner back to his cell.

(to guards)

And you—follow me.

(He leaves by the door at the rear.)

COCONNAS

(going to the side door so as to be in the way of the jailor)

A moment, friend! You know our agreements?

LA MÔLE

(to jailor)

You recall what you promised me?

COCONNAS

A meeting with my friend, La Môle.

LA MÔLE

And interview with the count.

JAILOR

It's true.

COCONNAS

Well, since we are reunited, let us alone to talk together.

JAILOR

Go ahead, sir—only for your sake as much as mine, don't talk politics.

COCONNAS

By God! Rest easy—we have much better things to tell each other.

JAILOR

In the meantime, I am going to keep watch so that you won't be surprised any more than I.

COCONNAS

Go, brave man!

(searching his pockets)

The first time you meet the governor, ask him for my three crowns.

LA MÔLE

When I arrived, he was searching you it seemed to me.

COCONNAS

Oh, My God, yes.

LA MÔLE

And he took everything from you?

COCONNAS

Everything! My all wasn't very much!

LA MÔLE   —

Now, do you understand what's happening to us?

COCONNAS

Perfectly.

LA MÔLE

We've been betrayed.

COCONNAS

By this frightful Duke d'Alençon.

LA MÔLE

And you think our affair is very grave?

COCONNAS

I am afraid so.

LA MÔLE

Have they questioned you?

COCONNAS

Yes and you?

LA MÔLE

I, too—but a strange thing—they've hardly asked me anything about the King of Navarre or Queen Marguerite.

COCONNAS

Exactly—and that's what very much astonishes me—all the questions revolved around this nasty wax doll—they insist it must be a portrait of the king.

LA MÔLE

You haven't told them it was of Madame Marguerite?

COCONNAS

No.

LA MÔLE

What did you say?

COCONNAS

Nothing—I laughed in their faces.

LA MÔLE

Dear Hannibal?

COCONNAS

Listen, it appears that we have, even in our prison, an invisible protector.

LA MÔLE

I was going to tell you.

COCONNAS

You've noticed it?

LA MÔLE

Yes, but you—

COCONNAS

Listen, this morning I heard scratching at my door and I saw a letter passed underneath.

LA MÔLE

This morning a stone fell in my cell—and I found a letter attached to this stone.

COCONNAS

The letter was from Madame de Nevers and contained only one line—"Be at ease, dear Hannibal—I love you."

LA MÔLE

This letter was from Madame Marguerite and it contained these words, "Good courage, I am watching."

COCONNAS

And do you know who was able to bring us these letters?

LA MÔLE

No.

COCONNAS

By God! I still really would like to know.

JAILOR

(entering)

Want me to tell you?

LA MÔLE and COCONNAS

(separating)

Ah—

JAILOR

It was me.

LA MÔLE

What—it was you?

JAILOR

Yes.

COCONNAS

Who brought to each a letter?

JAILOR

Yes.

COCONNAS

To me—on behalf of—

JAILOR

Of Madame the Duchess of de Nevers.

LA MÔLE

And to me?

JAILOR

On behalf of Madam Marguerite.

COCONNAS

And that means—

JAILOR

It means one cannot refuse anything to two great princesses.

LA MÔLE

You've seen them?

JAILOR

Doubtless.

COCONNAS

When was that?

JAILOR

Yesterday.

LA MÔLE

How?

JAILOR

We all get off once a week.

COCONNAS

God! I wish I could say as much.

JAILOR

Yesterday was my day of leave.

LA MÔLE

Hurry up! Hurry up!

JAILOR

A veiled woman was waiting for me at the door. She gave me a sign to follow her. I hesitated—she showed me a purse.

COCONNAS

That's precisely it. Iron follows the lover, and man follows gold. Go on—

JAILOR

I followed her. She brought me to the Hotel de Guise.

LA MÔLE

To the Hotel de Guise?

COCONNAS

Without a doubt, to the Hotel de Guise. There our two princesses were waiting—right?

JAILOR

Yes—and in fact, even in tears.

LA MÔLE

Dear Queen.

COCONNAS

And as you are very sensitive, you did not resist their tears, right, brave fellow?

JAILOR

Ah, sir, how you know me.

LA MÔLE

Well—what has been decided?

JAILOR

It was decided that tonight you will prepare to flee.

COCONNAS

Good.

JAILOR

Thanks to me, the two princesses have been introduced into your prison.

LA MÔLE

Here? They consented?

COCONNAS

And I know their feelings, by God! There are situations where you cannot be proud and then? For it's not important they get in here—the important thing is we are going to get out of here.

JAILOR

And then—since I have the keys I will escort you to the chapel through some empty corridors. This chapel has a door which gives on a park—at this door three horses will be waiting.

LA MÔLE

Why three? One of the two will follow us?

JAILOR

No—but I follow you.

COCONNAS

Marvelous, my brave man! Come—come I ask nothing better than to see you at fifty leagues from Vincennes—and me too. And the horses will be good, I hope.

JAILOR

The best from Madame de Nevers' stables.

COCONNAS

I know them—bravo!

JAILOR

Other relays are echeloned on the route. In twelve hours, you will reach Lorraine.

COCONNAS

Ah! We are going to Lorraine?

JAILOR

Have you something against Lorraine?

COCONNAS

Not at all! It's a charming county so I've heard at least—not counting its frontier is the closest to the frontier of France—which is not to be despised.

LA MÔLE

Oh! It's a magnificent plan.

COCONNAS

An escape which will do us the greatest honor. This brave Henriette, I am sure she's the one who planned this.

LA MÔLE

Dear Queen.

JAILOR

And now gentlemen, forget nothing of what I have told you.

(The jailor exits.)

COCONNAS

(striking his forehead)

Be easy, that's it.

(to La Môle)

This thing must have cost them dear—but, my word, they are not and will never have a better use for their money.

LA MÔLE

Oh, my friend, my friend, we are going to see them again.

COCONNAS

Yes—then, with them, the fields, the countryside, the woods. I have never felt so much taste for the rustic things. Oh—the best thing is fear—but fear in the open spaces, when you have a sword at your side, when you shout hurrah at your horse and you spur him on, and at each hurrah! he leaps and runs.

JAILOR

(rushing in)

Eh quick—eh! Quick? de La Môle—they are making their way to your cell. Go back. Go back!

COCONNAS

Some new deviltry of Queen Catherine or Monsieur d'Alençon. In any case, until this evening.

LA MÔLE

Till this evening, friend!

(La Môle and the jailor exit.)

COCONNAS

(alone)

By God! What a plaguey existence. Always extremes, never firm earth. You wade in a hundred feet of water or soar above the waves. Let's see—where are we? What's coming here? No—it appears it is not with me they have an affair. But as we have committed the same crime meaning we are both innocent, it is probable that whatever happens to one will happen to the other. Oh, what is that? It seems to me that I heard something like a—

(he hears a low moan)

Doubtless the cry of the wind which weeps in the corridors of this old chateau—without a doubt—no, no—it's indeed a human voice—

(another shriek)

And that voice—my God—that voice—

(rushing against the door)

It seemed to me it was that of La Môle.

(a moment of silence during which a new shout can be heard)

But are they butchering someone here—? Oh! Passage of arms—passage of arms.

(the door at the rear opens)

At least, I am going to know what is going on.

(A judge enters, a Clerk of Court, then Caboche followed by his assistants.)

JUDGE

The accused Mark Hannibal de Coconnas, you are to hear the charges be read against you.

COCONNAS

Ah—I breathe.

CLERK OF COURT

Accused. On your knees.

COCONNAS

On my knees?

(Two assistants pass behind him and force him to his knees.)

ASSISTANTS

Yes, on your knees.

CLERK OF COURT

"Arrest ordered by the Court sitting at Vincennes, seized and convicted for poisoning, witchcraft, and magic against the person of the King—and conspiracy against the security of the state. In consequence whereof, the said Mark Hannibal Coconnas is to be conducted from his prison to the Place Saint Jean de Grève to be decapitated; his estates confiscated; his woods of high forests cut to the height of six feet; his chateau destroyed and in the high places a post will be erected with a plaque which will memorialize the crime and the punishment."

COCONNAS

As to my head, I think that they will sever it, for it is in France, and that's very risky, as for my forests of high trees and my chateau, I defy all the pick axes and scythes of this very Christian kingdom to bite them down.

JUDGE

Silence! Continue, Clerk.

CLERK OF COURT

Moreover, the said Coconnas will be—

COCONNAS

What! More is to be done to me after my head's chopped off at the Place de Grève? On, oh, now that seems to me to be very severe.

JUDGE

No, sir, but the proceeding that—

CLERK OF COURT

"And moreover, the said Coconnas will be—before the execution of the judgment subjected to the Extraordinary Question."

COCONNAS

Torture! And for doing what?

CLERK OF COURT

"In order to force him to reveal his accomplices, his conspiracies and machinations in detail."

COCONNAS

By God! That's what I call infamous! Indeed, it's more than infamous—it's what I call cowardice.

JUDGE

(to Caboche's assistants)

Proceed!

COCONNAS

Proceed with what?

JUDGE

In accordance with the terms of the warrant.

(They strip Coconnas, stretch him on a chair employed in the question and garrotte him.)

COCONNAS

Wretches! Torture me, break me, tear me to shreds. Ah! You think with little pieces of wood and iron you can make a gentleman of my name speak? Go on, go on, I defy you.

JUDGE

Prepare to write, Clerk.

JUDGE

Will you make these revelations?

COCONNAS

Go to the devil!

JUDGE

Very well, master, adjust the gentleman's boots.

(Caboche approaches slowly and impassively. Coconnas watches him as if he saw a ghost.)

COCONNAS

Oh! It's you?

JUDGE

(to Caboche)

Begin!

(Caboche attaches boards to Coconnas' limbs and prepares some wedges. To Coconnas)

JUDGE

Will you speak?

COCONNAS

No.

JUDGE

First wedge in the usual way.

(Caboche lifts his hammer, strikes the wedge which slides between the planks. Coconnas' face expresses only surprise and not the least pain.)

JUDGE

Is the wedge driven in as far as it will go, Master?

CABOCHE

As far as it will go, sir.

JUDGE

Here's a tough Christian.

CABOCHE

(bending down to look)

But cry out, you unhappy man.

COCONNAS

(aside)

Ah—I understand—worthy Caboche, go!—Yes, yes, be easy, I will cry since you order me—and if you are not content, you're very hard to please.

JUDGE

What was your intention in hiding yourself in the forest?

COCONNAS

(joking)

To sit down in the shade.

JUDGE

Second wedge.

(Caboche forces the wedge in.)

COCONNAS

Ah! Ah! Oh! Oh! Take care! You are breaking my bones.

(to Caboche)

Is that better?

CABOCHE

Yes, not bad!

JUDGE

Ah, this one is having its effect. What were you doing in the forest?

COCONNAS

Eh! By God! I just told you. I was taking the air.

CABOCHE

(low)

Confess!

COCONNAS

(low)

What?

CABOCHE

(low)

Whatever you like; but confess something.

(He raises his hammer.)

COCONNAS

No, no, it's not necessary—what do you wish to know, Your

Honor?

JUDGE

What had you come to do in the forest?

COCONNAS

I came to assist the flight of the Duke d'Alençon. Ah, you denounce us, pale face. Wait! Wait!

JUDGE

Let us leave the Duke d'Alençon and return to the King of Navarre. What do you know of the flight of the King of Navarre?

COCONNAS

All I know is that Duke d'Alençon had a rendezvous with Monsieur de Mouy, that Monsieur d'Alençon had rounded up some Huguenots to flee with them, that Monsieur d'Alençon.

JUDGE

Enough. We are not investigating the Duke d'Alençon—we are investigating the King of Navarre—what do you know about the King of Navarre?

COCONNAS

Ah, the King of Navarre is another matter. I know nothing of him.

JUDGE

What do you know of the wax figure found by Monsieur de La

Môle?

COCONNAS

I know nothing about it.

JUDGE

What do you know about Queen Marguerite?

COCONNAS

I know nothing about her.

(At each reply, Caboche hammers in another wedge.)

JUDGE

Well, master.

CABOCHE

My work is done, sir and I think the accused cannot take anymore.

JUDGE

(dictating)

And, the accused, despite the Ordinary Question and the Extraordinary Question administered to him in our presence, refused to reply, we have closed the present interrogation" and now, master the accused belongs to you—it's your business and God's.

(The judge retires with his suite.)

CABOCHE

(after watching them all leave)

Well, sir, how do you feel?

COCONNAS

Ah, my friend, my brave Caboche, I will never forget what you just did for me.

CABOCHE

And you would be right sir, for if they knew what I just did for you, I would be taking your place—and they wouldn't manage things for me the way I did for you.

COCONNAS

So your wedges—?

CABOCHE

Are iron in appearance, and in reality, wax.

COCONNAS

That's rather ingenious! But where did you get the idea?

CABOCHE

(loosening the apparatus)

There! I knew you had been arrested, I knew they'd investigate you—I knew that Queen Catherine wished your death—I knew you'd be put to the Question, and I took precautions as a consequence.

COCONNAS

At the risk of what might happen to you?

CABOCHE

Sir, you are the only gentleman who ever shook my hand, and one has a memory and a heart, executioner though I am, and perhaps because I am executioner. You will see tomorrow how I do my work.

COCONNAS

Tomorrow?

CABOCHE

Tomorrow—without a doubt.

COCONNAS

What work?

CABOCHE

What! Have you forgotten?

COCONNAS

Ah! That's true! It's tomorrow—oh—hell!

CABOCHE

(to Coconnas who is ready to rise)

What are you doing? Take care—my helpers are about; they must believe you have broken limbs—at each move you make let out a scream.

COCONNAS

(to the assistants)

Eh! Take care! Touch me as if I was made of glass. Yi! By God! Yi! Take care, will you—oh—oh—

(to Caboche)

Caboche, my friend—

(He grips Caboche's hand.)

TURNKEY

(a lantern in hand)

Put the prisoner against this wall.

COCONNAS

Good! It's our turnkey—won't I have the consolation of being reunited with my companion?

TURNKEY

They're bringing him.

COCONNAS

Fine, put him there—facing me.

(They bring in La Môle and place him facing Coconnas.)

CABOCHE

Be of good courage, sir! Till tomorrow.

COCONNAS

(low)

Tomorrow! I hope indeed to be out of your claws tomorrow.

CABOCHE

Till we meet again.

COCONNAS

Goodbye! Goodbye! Plague—he is charming. Till we meet again. There, that's fine. Get out, shut the door—two locks rather than one.

(to Turnkey)

No, friend—have you heard of our princesses?

TURNKEY

They are there, in a nearby cell.

COCONNAS

(rising)

And you made them wait, wretch! Quick, quick! Think that the sooner they are here, the sooner we will be out of here—open,

open, friend.

(The turnkey opens the door.)

MADAME DE NEVERS

(entering)

Dear Hannibal.

MARGUERITE

(entering)

La Môle, my friend!

LA MÔLE

(with a cry)

Ah! My God!

MARGUERITE

What's the matter then?

COCONNAS

Come, come, not a moment to lose. La Môle—the horses are—there!

MARGUERITE

(terrified)

Oh! Blood!

COCONNAS

Blood! What did they do to you?

LA MÔLE

Wasn't it in the warrant that we be tortured?

COCONNAS

Didn't they do for you what they did to me?

LA MÔLE

I don't know what was done to you, but I know I have broken legs.

MARGUERITE

Mercy of God!

JAILOR

Let's go, let's go, gentleman. Don't lose any time, the rain is falling. The wind whistling and the horses are impatient. They could be seen by a night patrol.

MARGUERITE

What's to be done? My God? My God? Inspire us.

COCONNAS

Come, friend, courage! I am strong, I will carry you. I will place you on your horse, I will hold you in front of me, if you cannot sit in the saddle, but let's go—let's go. You clearly understood what this brave man said—it's a question of life.

LA MÔLE

It's true, it's a question of life. Let us try.

(after an effort and a cry)

Ah, impossible! Impossible!

MARGUERITE

Henriette! Henriette! What's to be done—what will happen? Oh! My God! To be rich, to be Queen, to be powerful and to suffer—to suffer like this.

LA MÔLE

Courage, my Queen. You, Hannibal, since you've been spared suffering, you are young, you are loved, you can live—flee—flee—my friend, flee and leave me the supreme consolation of knowing you are at liberty.

JAILOR

The time passes—time passes—hurry!

LA MÔLE

Flee, Hannibal—flee! Don't give our enemies the joyous spectacle of two innocents' death. Flee, I beg you.

MADAME DE NEVERS

Come, Hannibal, come.

COCONNAS

First, Madame, give this man what you promised him.

(pointing to the jailor)

MADAME DE NEVERS

(drawing a purse)

There!

COCONNAS

And now, good La Môle, you do me injury in thinking for a moment that I can abandon you. Didn't I swear to live and die with you? But you suffer so much that I pardon you.

MADAME DE NEVERS

What are you saying, Hannibal?

COCONNAS

I say, Madame, they have broken his legs and that he cannot mount the scaffold without a friend to carry him—and that I will carry him.

MADAME DE NEVERS

My Hannibal! Another woman would pray, would beg, but I, I understand you and I am proud of you—Hannibal before God, I will always love you above all else—and more than all else—I promise you, I swear to you.

COCONNAS

That was bravely spoken, Madame—thanks!

JAILOR

They are coming, they are coming.

LA MÔLE

Before leaving us, my Queen, a last grace. Give me some remembrance of you that I can kiss on mounting the scaffold.

MARGUERITE

Oh, yes—here!

(detaching a reliquary from her neck and giving it to him)

Here—here's a holy relic that I've worn since childhood—I have never parted from it—take it—take it.

JAILOR

They are opening the door. Flee, Madame, flee!

COCONNAS

(taking Marguerite's hand and placing it in La Môle's)

Goodbye here, till you meet above.

MARGUERITE, MME DE NEVERS

(in tears)

Goodbye! Goodbye!

(The two women flee by a side door. The two men follow them with their eyes, arms extended towards them. The door in the rear opens—a priest and guards can be seen to enter.)

CURTAIN

ACT IV
SCENE 12

The Executioner's House.

Joylette elbows on the table is weeping.

CABOCHE

(entering)

This is the first time I've come in that she didn't jump on my neck. She heard the door open and she's recognized my step— Joylette!

JOYLETTE

(shuddering)

Huh?

CABOCHE

What are you doing there?

JOYLETTE

Nothing, father!

CABOCHE

Are you crying!

JOYLETTE

Alas!

CABOCHE

Come, my child.

JOYLETTE

Father.

(going to him)

It is true that the handsome gentleman who, one day came to see you to thank you, who shook your hand, who embraced me—is it true that he is dead?

CABOCHE

Who told you that?

JOYLETTE

They told me.

CABOCHE

I forbade you to go out today. Did you disobey?

JOYLETTE

No father. I heard the judgment proclaimed and I recognized the name.

CABOCHE

Yes, it's true.

JOYLETTE

He is dead! Poor young man!

CABOCHE

But, now he's blessing me in heaven for I spared him all pain. Yesterday, when you asked me what these wax wedges were for, I didn't tell you. It was for him.

JOYLETTE

And his companion?

CABOCHE

Oh! That's another matter; his companion didn't shake my hand—come on, Joylette, let's not talk about it anymore.

JOYLETTE

What's the use of not speaking of it anymore? We will always think about it.

CABOCHE

Set the table. After supper, I have to go out.

JOYLETTE

Where are you going, father?

CABOCHE

To the Louvre. The youngest of the two charged me with a commission for a great lady. I promised him to do it, and I will do it.

JOYLETTE

My God! My God!

(Someone knocks.)

CABOCHE

Someone's knocking. Silence.

JOYLETTE

Who would come to us—where no one comes?

CABOCHE

(looking through a peephole)

Two women.

(opening the door)

Enter!

(Marguerite and Mme. de Nevers, both veiled, enter.)

MARGUERITE

(raising a veil)

Do you recognize me, master?

CABOCHE

Yes, Madame, it's you who made me come to the Louvre for a wounded man.

MARGUERITE

It's me—well, this gentleman—I made him a promise and I've come to accomplish it.

CABOCHE

I was going to the Louvre to remind you.

MARGUERITE

There's no need of that, master; I have a memory.

CABOCHE

Come!

MARGUERITE

One moment—you didn't leave them, right?

CABOCHE

No.—from Vincennes to La Grève.

MARGUERITE

What did they do? What did they say? It's frightful, I realize that, but my friend and I, we must know this.

MADAME DE NEVERS

(under her veil)

Yes—speak—speak.

JOYLETTE

Poor ladies. They loved them!

CABOCHE

First of all—down there, as de La Môle could not walk, his friend took him in his arms as if he were a child. When the people saw them, both so young, both so handsome, brothers in pain, the strong carrying the weak—the weak consoling the strong—then—there had not been, the entire length of the route, anything but complaints, lamentations for these wretches and curses against those who killed them.

MARGUERITE, MME DE NEVERS

My God! My God!

CABOCHE

Count de Coconnas said to me, "Don't you have some cordial, master? My friend is fainting with pain and I do not want anyone to think it is with fear." So, I gave him a flask of elixir; the other one drank several drops and came to himself. Then he fervently kissed a relic that hung from his neck and said, 'My God—all powerful father, I believe in you—and I hope we will meet in heaven those who loved us on earth."

MARGUERITE, MME DE NEVERS

Oh! Yes! Oh! Yes!

CABOCHE

Arriving at the Place de Grève, noticing the scaffold, the youngest one said, 'Friend, I want to die first—' that's fine, that's fine, I told him, I understood. "And by a single blow, right," added Coconnas. "If you must take your time, take your time with me."

MADAME DE NEVERS

Brave Hannibal.

CABOCHE

We stopped. Ah, Madame, there were only tears and weeping around us. "You promised to carry me," said La Môle. "Yes, yes, rest assured!" replied de Coconnas. And he took him in his arms as he had already done—and he mounted. The scaffold without help from anyone—or rather without wanting anyone to touch him—only, the one who was being carried said, 'Look carefully, Hannibal—look carefully around us—I am sure that we are going to see them again." In fact, when he was placed on the platform he extended his hand toward the little turret which is found in the corner of the square and pointed to two women dressed in black—who were embracing and wept.

(The two women embrace and weep)

Then his friend said to him, "Embrace me, La Môle, and die

well—it will not be difficult for you, friend, you are so brave!"
"Ah," said de La Môle—there's no merit in my dying well—I am
in so much pain at the moment." The oldest gave me a sign—I
understood. Oh, Madame, in the name of the Virgin, since you
saw everything, have pity on me.

MARGUERITE

No, no, not a word more—you are right—where are they?

CABOCHE

There—lying next to each other—hand-in-hand.

MARGUERITE

We want to see them, maser, for we made a promise to the living
that we must keep with the dead.

CABOCHE

(drawing a large curtain)

Come!

(The two friends can be seen lying next to each other in the
horrible symmetry of death. They are covered with a cape which
doesn't allow their heads to be seen. The two women approach
religiously and kiss their faces.)

MARGUERITE

La Môle! Dear La Môle!

MADAME DE NEVERS

Hannibal! Hannibal! So handsome, so proud, so brave! Alas! Alas! I call you and you do not answer.

JOYLETTE

(on her knees)

My God! My God! Give strength to those who are suffering—have pity on those who weep.

MARGUERITE

Now—

MADAME DE NEVERS

(pulling a ruby necklace from her throat)

You will pray for their souls. Goodbye, Master, goodbye, come, Marguerite, come.

(Caboche shuts the curtain. The two women make an effort and disappear.)

JOYLETTE

Father, I ask you for the smallest ruby from this necklace.

CABOCHE

What will you use it for, my child?

JOYLETTE

To pay my dowry at the Convent of the Daughters of Calvary—
which I beg you on my knees for permission to enter—tomorrow.

CURTAIN

ACT V
SCENE 13

The King's bedchamber in the Château of Vincennes. In a corner, an office whose interior can be seen—in the distance a large window with a balcony.

The King is praying, the Nurse is near the door.

KING

My Lord, God, pardon me! My Lord, God—have pity on me.

(praying)

CATHERINE

(comes into the office leading Maureval by the hand)

Stay here, Maureval—the King is getting worse and worse—and if he dies, perhaps I will have instant need of you—

MAUREVAL

Your Majesty knows I am at her orders with the entire regiment of arquebusiers of which she made me the captain.

CATHERINE

And where are your people?

MAUREVAL

In the courtyard of the Château.

CATHERINE

And the King of Navarre is guarded, right?

MAUREVAL

He is in the dungeon, with two men in his room and six others at the door.

CATHERINE

Oh—don't let him scheme with news from outside. de Maureval, don't let him flee—you will answer for him?

MAUREVAL

Fear nothing, Madame.

KING

(praying)

Oh, my God! My God! Lord—if you will that I die, call me to you immediately, my God—Oh! Help me! Help me! Call for help. This blood is flowing. Ambrose Paré! Help!

NURSE

Aid to the King! Aid to the King! Help! Help! The King is dying.

DE NANCEY, COURTIERS

The King—the King.

NURSE

Call Master Ambrose Paré—Master Ambrose! Ah! My Charles!

KING

This blood—this blood—

(noticing Catherine)

Pardon, Madame, but I should like to die in peace.

CATHERINE

To die, my son! From an attack of this villainous illness! Why do you despair so?

KING

I tell you, Madame, that I feel my soul leaving. I tell you, Madame, that death is coming. Oh, I know what I feel, I know what I'm talking about.

CATHERINE

Sire, your imagination is your worst illness. Since the well-deserved sacrifice of those two sorcerers, of those two murderers, called La Môle and Coconnas, your physical pains ought to have diminished—the moral evil alone perseveres, and if I could only talk with you for 10 minutes I would prove to you—

KING

You think so? Well—Leave gentlemen—and you, Nurse, watch at the door. Queen Catherine de Medici wishes to talk with her well-beloved son, Charles the IX. Only, Madame, a third person must assist in this conversation.

CATHERINE

And who is the third person you wish to see?

KING

My brother, Madame. Have him called.

CATHERINE

Nurse, by the order of the King—tell Monsieur de Nancey to get the Duke d'Alençon.

KING

No, not the Duke d'Alençon—I said my brother, Madame.

CATHERINE

And of which brother do you mean to speak?

KING

I mean to speak of Henry and not the Duke d'Anjou nor the Duke d'Alençon, Henry of Navarre is my brother, Henry of

Navarre alone will know my last wishes.

CATHERINE

Henry of Navarre. And, I, do you think Charles, if you are as near the tomb as you say, do you believe that I will cede to anyone, especially a stranger—the right to assist you in your last hour—that right which is my right as Queen—my right as mother.

KING

You are no more my mother, Madame, any more than the Duke d'Alençon is my brother.

CATHERINE

Since when is she who gives birth not the mother of the child she bore?

KING

From the moment, Madame, that this unnatural mother took the life she gave.

CATHERINE

What do you mean? I do not understand you.

KING

You will understand me.

(taking a little gold key from under his holster)

Take this key, Madame, and open that casket—it contains some papers which will speak for me.

CATHERINE

(opening the box and recoiling)

Oh!

KING

Well—what's in this box that frightens you, Madame? Speak, Madame, speak.

CATHERINE

Nothing.

KING

In that case, plunge your hand in and bring out a book. There must be a book there, right?

CATHERINE

Yes.

KING

A book on hunting?

CATHERINE

Yes.

KING

Take it and bring it to me.

CATHERINE

(taking the book)

Calamity!

KING

Fine—listen now—this book—I was senseless—I liked hunting more than anything—this hunting book—I read it—do you understand?

CATHERINE

Oh! My God! My God!

KING

It was a weakness. Burn it, Madame. The weaknesses of Kings must not be known.

(Catherine takes the book to the fireplace)

And now, Madame, call my brother.

CATHERINE

(going to the office)

Oh—may he be cursed!

KING

You hear—my brother, Henry of Navarre, to whom I wish to speak right now on the subject of the Regency of the Kingdom.

CATHERINE

(in the office to Maureval)

Monsieur de Maureval—how long will it take for a well mounted horseman to leave for Vincennes?

MAUREVAL

Five minutes, Madame.

CATHERINE

Do you have horses ready?

MAUREVAL

Yes.

CATHERINE

Run to the dungeon—open the gates—escort the King of Navarre to the esplanade let him mount a horse so that in five minutes he will be free and outside the chateau.

MAUREVAL

Madame!

CATHERINE

I am going to release my son Francis, and I am coming back here—In five minutes—neither more nor less—you understand me?

(They, Maureval and the Queen Mother, leave.)

NURSE

(bringing a drink)

Well, my Charles, how do you feel?

KING

Better, much better, nurse. It's better to go at the approach of death when one suffers as I do. Always this sweating of blood! Always!

NURSE

Ah—it's the blood of the Huguenots, poor Charles.

KING

You think so? It's possible—but my mother, my brother, de Guise shed much more than I.

NURSE

Yes, but it's you, my child, it's you who authorized them to shed it. Ah, I said it, I told you so.

KING

Enough, Nurse! Pray—pray—there are already too many voices around me cursing—but Little Henry isn't coming—I don't have long to wait—Henry! Henry!

CATHERINE

Sire, the King of Navarre's not coming.

KING

Why's that, Madame?

CATHERINE

Because this good Henry—this beloved brother, this faithful friend, finding himself ill at ease under the same roof as Your Majesty, because he prefers his conspiracies to your Protection, his rebels in Navarre, because he's just fled from Vincennes and at this hour is rejoining his Huguenots, his fine allies.

KING

Henry in flight—he who asked me to remain here? Henry a traitor? Henry abandoning me? Oh—this last blow finishes me. Little Henry—Little Henry—Henry, be cursed Henry—Henry—

HENRY

(entering during this last words)

You called me, brother?

CATHERINE

The Bernese!

KING

Henry! Ah—you see, Madame.

(Overcome by this effort, the King falls back in his armchair—and loses consciousness.)

CATHERINE

(seizing Henry's arm)

What have you come to do here?

HENRY

When you kept me prisoner, I tried to flee, Madame, but today when you offer me liberty through the intervention of de Maureval, I understood that I must stay in Vincennes, so I let Monsieur de Maureval open the door for me, but I am returning and I am staying here.

CATHERINE

You came to speak to the King?

HENRY

I've come to see my brother, who is sick, that they tell me is dying.

CATHERINE

(with irony)

Faithful friend! Tender relative! You have no other design?

HENRY

To be King—haven't you a heart, haven't you some tears before suffering like this?

(pointing to the King)

CATHERINE

Listen, sir, we haven't time to lend to your sensitivity or your tricks. Let's play our game as King and Queen. If you have some ambition, if you are allowed to see the King, if you were made an offer?

HENRY

What offer do you want him to make me, Madame?

CATHERINE

I don't know, but if he makes one—and you accepted it—

HENRY

Well?

CATHERINE

Reflect!

HENRY

Since I am playing this royal gamble with you, Madame, I've had time to reflect.

(The King awakens little by little, he listens and observes.)

CATHERINE

Well, through this door through which you entered, by this door you must leave to find life and liberty—unless you've given in to ambition.

HENRY

And if I am ambitious?

CATHERINE

Then I will be at this door.

(She pulls from his hand and draws a dagger.)

KING

(seizing the dagger from Catherine)

Go through here, Little Henry!

HENRY

(throwing himself on the King's hand)

My King!

CATHERINE

(enraged)

Oh!

KING

You, Madame, leave us.

CATHERINE

But what you are going to say to the King of Navarre? I still must know.

KING

In effect, you already know it; I will call you, Madame, when it is time. You may await my orders.

CATHERINE

(leaving)

If Maureval is not used to freeing prisoners at least, do him justice—he kills them.

(She exits.)

KING

(dismissing the Nurse with a gesture)

You love me then—Henry? You?

HENRY

With all my heart, Sire.

KING

Oh! Henry, how I suffered from not seeing you. I tortured you so much in my life, my poor friend.

HENRY

Sire, I remember only the love I bore my king.

KING

Thanks, Little Henry—for you have suffered so much under my reign—under my reign, where your mother died.

HENRY

Let's not speak of the past, Sire.

KING

The present is hardly mine, and the future no longer belongs to me. I am dying, do you see, Henry! I am dying.

HENRY

Don't speak of that, my brother, full of youth, full of strength still—powerful king of the most beautiful realm on earth—you die? Oh! Not at all—you will live.

KING

Henry, perhaps they told you that I am sweating at every pore, the blood of the Huguenots killed on St. Bartholomew! Well, it's not their blood—it's poison which is escaping from my veins.

HENRY

Poison? Oh! Sire, tell me who the murderers are!

KING

Silence, Henry! If my death is to be avenged it's by God alone! Let's not speak any more of me. I am dead, I tell you.

(The King goes to an armchair.)

HENRY

Sire, you will be saved.

KING

Impossible—and why should I still live? To put up with all these traitors, all these assassins who surrounded me, to assist in the agony of France, to see my once so beautiful crown fall to pieces, bit by bit. No, I prefer to die completely, to die King.

HENRY

Hunt out the murderers! Destroy the traitors! The crown slides from your head, you say!

KING

Raise your head. All is finished.

HENRY

This corrupted nobility—degraded, betrayed by Italian intrigues—sweep it out! Extend the hand to year true friends, who massacred by their king spill yet more tears than blood. Give parliament its rights, to the people freedom, the day you have magistrates instead of courtiers, fellow citizens instead of slaves, a happy people instead of famished subjects—that day you will insist on living—kings are very strong when they are loved.

KING

It's you who say this, Henry!

HENRY

It's I who would do it, sire, if I were the master.

KING

You will do it.

HENRY

My King!

KING

It's very necessary that I make you strong to resist these implacable enemies that I leave you—Monsieur d'Alençon, my mother, you accept, right?

(Noise of arms in the antechamber.)

HENRY

(to himself)

Oh—what's that noise?

KING

You are afraid? You hesitate?

HENRY

No, Sire, I am not afraid, no, Sire, I do not hesitate anymore. I accept.

KING

That's well—Nurse, call my mother. Then have Monsieur d'Alençon come.

NURSE

They are there waiting.

KING

Let them enter.

(Catherine and Monsieur d'Alençon enter.)

CATHERINE

Here we are, what do you want of us, Sire?

KING

Madame, I wish to tell you that I have chosen a regent who can take on deposit, the crown and who can protect it under his hand and not on his head. This regent—salute him, brother. This regent is the King of Navarre. Here, Regent, here's the parchment which until the return of the King of Poland, gives you command of the army, the key to the treasury, the prerogatives and royal powers.

(Catherine makes a motion.)

KING

Ah! You don't answer—? You don't obey?

CATHERINE

No, I don't answer—no, I won't obey—for never will my race bow its head to a foreign race. Never will a Bourbon reign in France so long as there remains one Valois.

KING

Madame—it doesn't take much time to give an order. It doesn't take much time to punish murderers and poisoners..

CATHERINE

Well, give this order if you dare. While waiting, I'm going to give mine. Come, my son.

(She leaves, pulling d'Alençon after her.)

KING

Nancey! Nancey! Help. I order it! I wish it. Nancey, arrest my mother—and my brother. They are the ones who—ah—

(The King falls into a faint, chocked on blood. They carry him to his bed.)

HENRY

(to Monsieur de Nancey)

Guard the door, sir, and don't let anyone enter.

DE NANCEY

But in whose name do you give me this order, Sire?

HENRY

(showing him the parchment)

In my name. I am Regent of France. Here's the last moment. Will he live? Will he reign?

(De Nancey bows and goes out.)

(A tapestry on the other side of the King's bed.)

RENÉ

He's going to live, Sire.

HENRY

René.

RENÉ

Yes, the prediction which said you will be King of France was
not false, but the hour has not come.

HENRY

How do you know? Can I believe you?

RENÉ

Listen.

HENRY

I am listening.

RENÉ

Lower your voice.

(Henry hesitates)

Do you suspect me?

HENRY

In my place, wouldn't you be suspicious? Speak.

RENÉ

Well—learn a secret.

HENRY

What?

RENÉ

A secret that I alone know and that I will reveal to you, if you swear by this dying man to pardon me for the death of your mother.

HENRY

All religious orders pardon. René on this dying man, I swear to pardon you.

RENÉ

Well, sire, the King of Poland is arriving.

HENRY

Oh, misfortune to me.

RENÉ

A messenger arrived this morning from Warsaw. He precedes King Henry of Anjou by only a few hours.

HENRY

Oh—if I only had eight hours.

RENÉ

Yes, but you don't have eight hours. Did you hear the clash of arms. They are preparing for him.

HENRY

Certainly.

RENÉ

Well, these arms are being prepared with you in mind. They will come to kill you even here, even in the King's room.

HENRY

The King is not dead yet.

RENÉ

No, but in five minutes he will be.

HENRY

What's to be done then?

RENÉ

Flee, escorted by four sure men.

HENRY

Are there four sure men for me in France?

DE MOUY

(appearing behind René)

Yes, Sire—they are commanded by me.

HENRY

De Mouy? Who let you in here?

DE MOUY

René.

RENÉ

Now, do you have confidence in me, Sire?

HENRY

Yes.

RENÉ

Well, follow me through this secret passage and I will escort you to the postern. Come! Come!

HENRY

(kissing Charles' face)

Goodbye my brother. Die in peace, poor abandoned man. In the name of our brothers, I pardon you—I will not forget that your last wish was for me to be king—Come gentlemen.

KING

(opening his eyes)

Nurse! Nurse!

(Henry leaves after having taken his sword from the bolster of the bed of the King. René and de Mouy follow him.)

Nurse! Nurse!

HENRY

Well, what's wrong, my Charles?

KING

Nurse! Something must have happened while I slept. I saw God who called me. My God! My God! Receive me in your mercy— My God, forget I was king—for I come to you without scepter and without crown—My God, forget the curses of the King so you may only remember the sufferings of man. My God! My God! Here I am—ah—

(he dies)

NURSE

Help! Help! The King is dead!

(Catherine, the Duke d'Alençon, De Nancey, courtiers, captains, enter.)

CATHERINE

Dead! All enter! Where is Henry? What has become of him?

(running to the balcony)

He's fleeing—he's fleeing! Wait—down there in the night with his brown cape with a white feather—fire, Monsieur de Maureval! Fire on the white plume!

(shots)

Ah—he falls—he's fallen—he's dead. Bring him here! Bring him here.

DUKE

He is dead! Then I am King.

MAUREVAL

Madame, the courtyard is full of guards, courtiers, and captains.

CATHERINE

Do what I told you, sir. Proclaim the Duke of Anjou!

DUKE

Stop, sir! My brother d'Anjou is in Poland and cannot be proclaimed king. My mother is mistaken.

CATHERINE

Your brother, d'Anjou is knocking at the gate of Vincennes this very moment, perhaps.

(the sound of trumpets can be heard)

Take care, my son, one word more and you are a rebel.

(They bring in a body enveloped in a brown cape. The face covered by a hat with a white feather.)

CATHERINE

Ah—there he is. There he is. Well, now where are the predictions of the astrologers who assured you of the kingdom of France—damned Bernese! Monsieur de Nancey, announce the death of the king and proclaim his successor.

DE NANCEY

(on the balcony)

King Charles is dead. King Charles is dead. King Charles is dead. Long live King Henry the Third!

DE MOUY

(rising the pulling off his cloak)

Long live Henry the Fourth.

(De Mouy falls back dead)

CATHERINE

Oh—it's the prophecy of the dead! He will reign. He will reign!

CURTAIN

ABOUT THE AUTHOR

Frank J. Morlock has written and translated many plays since retiring from the legal profession in 1992. His translations have also appeared on Project Gutenberg, the Alexandre Dumas Père web page, Literature in the Age of Napoléon, Infinite Artistries. com, and Munsey's (formerly Blackmask). In 2006 he received an award from the North American Jules Verne Society for his translations of Verne's plays. He lives and works in México.

15199924R00216

Printed in Poland
by Amazon Fulfillment
Poland Sp. z o.o., Wrocław